Peacemaking

Peacemaking

The Journey from Fear to Love

by Ronice E. Branding

CBP Press

St. Louis, Missouri

CBP Press
Box 179
St. Louis, MO 63166

Library of Congress Cataloging-in-Publication Data

Branding, Ronice E.
Peacemaking : the journey from fear to love.

1. Peace—Religious aspects—Christianity.
I. Title.
BT736.4.B685 1987 261.8'73 87-15829
ISBN 0-8272-2940-2

Printed in the United States of America

Contents

To Ron, whose love has been a constant through life's many changes,

To Kathy, Karen, Elaine, and Dave, whose love has given promise and delight;

To Mother, whose love continues to nourish;

To the memory of Dad, whose love taught me of the church.

Acknowledgments

In writing this book I have known joy and labor that is akin to that of bringing forth new life. In both, hope and energy are derived from the support of others, and it is difficult to imagine what it would be like to be alone. From the beginning of this effort I was blessed with the counsel, encouragement, and help of others. I want to acknowledge the significance of their support in bringing an idea to life.

I am grateful to Walter Brueggemann who, upon seeing the idea in its primal state, encouraged me to continue. As the content developed, I became aware of how much I have been affected by the witness of others who have written or taught by example about the faith dimensions of peace and justice. I am deeply indebted to these seekers and interpreters of truth. The congregational aspects of the book were shaped considerably by the experiences, needs, and reflections of clergy and laypersons working to find ways for churches to become peacemaking congregations. Perceptions on these matters were sharpened by the insights of an ecumenical and geographic mix of peacemakers who responded to my inquiries and survey. Application of theory was enriched by those participating in the "Peacemaking and the Congregation" section of the 1986 Summer Institute sponsored by the Institute for Peace and Justice at Eden Theological Seminary. The opportunity to propose an analysis and approach in a climate of sincerity and openness provided me with a wealth of ideas and information. I appreciate, too, that it has been possible to incorporate Brad Kent's contribution to that seminar within these pages.

To transfer substance into something that one hopes can become useful to others is not a solitary task. Kathy Knoke played a particular role in helping to make that happen. Her wisdom, honesty, and good humor prevailed over times of rewriting and beginning anew as she provided the necessary objective view, typing and editing in the process. I am privileged to have had her participation. I want to thank Herb Lambert, who believed enough in the idea to say yes to the publication of the work. Thanks also to Ann Currinder for her artistic gifts in creating a meaningful symbol for Christian peacemaking to use throughout the book.

The interest and support of friends and of co-workers at the Institute for Peace and Justice have meant a lot. I am grateful to the IPJ Shareholders whose support of the Institute made available to me time, office support, and the wonders of the word processor. Home routines throughout this endeavor have necessarily taken a different twist. I value the strengthening of my husband and family, who shared in the work with their adaptability, patience, and encouragement.

To each and everyone who has counseled, helped, shared, and encouraged—know that you have given the word *interdependence* a deeper meaning for my life. Thank you!

Ronice Branding
Florissant, Missouri

Foreword

It is odd but true that "peace" and "peacemaking" have become divisive and controversial matters in the American community, and even among American Christians. These words have become so vulnerable and elastic that they can be filled with a variety of ideological substances, including the most dangerous dreams of military domination and political control. Even if our language of ethics has become corrupted by our ideology, the urgency of peace questions will not go away. While our fear may for a long while yet justify our arms and our insistence on "peace through strength," such distortions will not finally lead to a human solution of our fearful situation.

Somewhere, sometime, sooner or later, there will have to be a break in the madness of our policies, in the pathology of our language, and in the cycles of fearfulness that shape our policies and our language. This book by Ronice Branding is about that urgent break that must, soon or late, change our public discussion and our personal discernment of our world. That urgent break with madness, pathology, and fearfulness is an awesome, scary, subversive task, but we eventually have no alternative. We can postpone that break awhile. But we cannot avoid it. Branding has invited us to think, pray, and live into that break that cannot finally be avoided.

There are a number of dimensions to this book that commend it in our pathological situation. First, Branding understands the complexity of the peace issue and understands the deep and undeniable link between personal feeling, world view, and public policy; between personal fear and public militarism. Thus her theme, "from fear to love," is an attempt to address the most elemental, prerational fears that we seldom acknowledge, but which drive and shape our common life. Her sense of this complexity is laid out with a shrewd and helpful analysis.

Second, Branding thinks theologically and understands that serious faith is a crucial ingredient of peacemaking. Branding is a child of the church and this lineage shows in her statement. As a result, her theological reflection is not ideological and abrasive, nor is it sweet and sentimental. Her faith tradition of genuine pietism has taught her the awareness of a God to whom our fears can be entrusted. And in such an act of trust we can be free for love that can impinge on public policy.

Third, Branding is a peaceable person. Her openness, candor, and irenic spirit come through in these pages. She knows from her work, but also from her day-to-day living, that peacemaking is not an occasional strategy, but it is a way of living. One is energized by her way of making the argument.

This book is an invitation that we not only acknowledge our madness and our pathology, for such an acknowledgment by itself is too dread-filled and immobilizes. It is also a thoughtful invitation to practical steps to peace. The outcome anticipated in this book is not simply admitting the problem, but accepting our God-given vocation as peacemakers.

I like the book on its own merits. I like it more because Roni has written it. After long years of friendship, it is a delight to thank her for the book. Her life in "Peace and Justice" is an enactment of the conviction that "perfect love casts out fear." Her conviction echoes a heritage of faith now powerfully important in our public destiny. This book can be a step for many of us from fear to love.

Walter Brueggemann
Columbia Theological Seminary

An Introduction

"It's gotten so you can't talk about peace without coming to blows!" This was the fearful response of a woman from a St. Louis congregation where some brave souls were trying to plan a study series on peacemaking. She had minced no words in summing up the fears and concerns of many who are reluctant participants to denominational policy statements on justice and peace.

Fears of conflict and polarization often preclude the struggle of how a congregation is to involve itself with the suffering Christ in Central America, South Africa, St. Louis, or Hometown, U.S.A. Fear about defense-related jobs and the opinions of others frequently serve as stoppers to Christians struggling with the difficult questions of faith that are posed by the arms race.

Indeed, the community of believers at times seems to be just as paralyzed by fear as those to whom we've been charged to bring hope. Christ's words of peace, hope, and justice are considered to be somewhere between irrelevant and terrifying—even foolish—to some when they are confronted with the morning paper.

But in spite of the fear and despair within the body of faith, there is an increasing number of the faithful in local congregations who are taking to heart Christ's call to peacemaking and social justice. Hardy are those peacemakers at the parish level who persevere at a task that often invites being lonely and misunderstood. Their efforts need to be recognized, celebrated, and supported. It has been my privilege to both teach and learn from an ecumenical range of these clergy and laypersons. I have found that their experiences, problems, and insights at the local level have much to offer others.

The difficulty of their task—which is in reality our task—poses some basic questions that this book seeks to address: Why is peacemaking, which some consider incidental to the life of the congregation, actually at the heart of the faith? Why does peacemaking frighten so many who claim to be followers of the Prince of Peace? How can fidelity to peacemaking strengthen the faith of the individual peacemaker, enrich the vitality of the congregation, and bear witness to the Good News? And finally, what exactly do we mean by a peacemaking congregation? How do hope, justice, and love funnel into ministry, program, and outreach?

As the questions may suggest, to be a Christian peacemaker or a peacemaking congregation encompasses far more than working to reverse the arms race or having a Lenten series on Central America. Christian peacemaking is birthed in the knowledge and acceptance of God's gift of grace. It is a journey that goes inward where hearts are disarmed of guilt and fear; it goes outward where relationships are reconciled and bonded, and to places where human systems and institutions are confronted with God's will for justice and peace.

This book is written in the hope that it will strengthen and support peacemakers, be they clergy or laity, in Christian congregations in the suburbs, in cities, and in rural America. May their efforts be blessed and fruitful. And may they know hope, joy, and the enabling power of the Holy Spirit as they seek to witness to the prophetic function of the Christian church.

Part I

Cycles of Brokenness

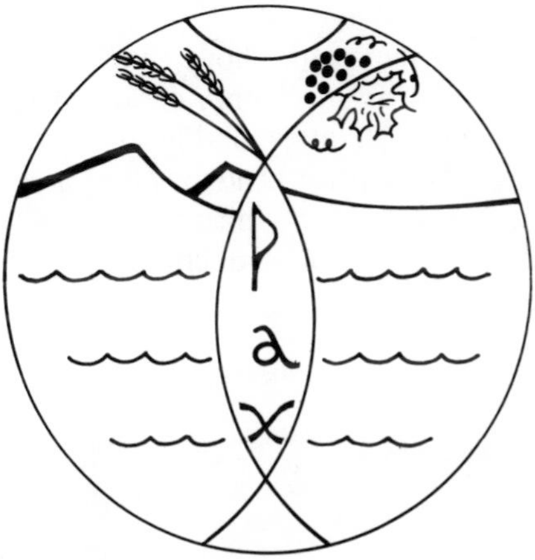

Part I

1

The Faces of Fear

fear: an unpleasant often strong emotion caused by anticipation or awareness of danger.

insecure: deficient in assurance: beset by fear and anxiety; not adequately guarded or sustained.[1]

We are a people living in a siege of fear. Fear has permeated nearly every facet of our daily living. Newspapers read like a litany of the fearful, with reports of international terrorism, nuclear accidents, polluted waters, and violent deaths. This is the public face of fear. Fear also takes its toll of the unseen and the unknown. For some who are experiencing the failure of a farm, the elimination of a job, the bizarre behavior of a loved one, or the loss of needed health care, relief from fearfulness does not seem to exist. Fear wears other faces as well, often a mask. Drugs and excesses in eating, working, and spending often provide a facade, behind which lurk fears of the spirit—fears of failure, rejection, or betrayal. This is but some of the sad evidence that fear and insecurity weigh heavily on the backs of our people. Added to the load is the often unspoken but ever-present fear of nuclear war and the total destruction of God's creation.

Fear has become more than a powerful human emotion. It is now an altar where people worship, sanctified by weapons and fortified walls. Nations and people alike have become its slave, handing over all power and authority. There is a striking paradox: Never have we spent so much to assure ourselves of security and peace of mind, and never have so many been so fearful. House alarms, tamper-resistant packaging, soaring insurance rates, bomb detectors, and computerized space weapons attest to both the real and perceived danger. Defensiveness has become a way of life, reinforced by the culture and reflected in our entertainment, advertising, and even our children's toys.

What is more disturbing is the hold that fear has on many congregations. "The LORD is my light and my salvation; I will fear no one. The LORD protects me from all danger; I will never be afraid" (Psalm 27:1). David's faith does not seem to be ours. For in spite of repeated scriptural reassurances to "fear not for I am with you," we are a worrisome lot; we even fear peacemaking! The courage of the bishops and other church leaders who have come out clearly against nuclear weapons and social injustice has not taken deep root in many mainline congregations. For some, the very words of peace and justice in the context of worship, meetings, budget, and outreach can be so threatening as to be avoided and closed out at all costs. That cost is a ransom of the faith.

In his book *Waging Peace*, Jim Wallis states that while the arms race has many complicated political and economic causes, its root cause is fear. "The bomb is the political result of fear. It is the logical and social extension of our personal fear and anxiety. We have allowed our faith and security in God to be overcome by fear, *the greatest enemy of faith and its final contradiction*." [emphasis added][2]

This assessment by a minister whose ecumenical leadership in the work for peace and justice has nurtured many, suggests that if we are to be peacemakers, we had better take a hard look at fear and the causes of our insecurity. To do so we need to look inward as well as outward, searching out the answers to some questions. What are our fears? How do they affect us? Theologian Walter Brueggemann has written that fear can be like the slavery of making bricks in Pharaoh's brickyard. It shackles and controls us, cutting us off from joy.[3] What happens when people are afraid? How does fear coerce us into doing what we don't want to do, and not doing what we would do? How can we be freed from fear to live lives of wholeness, freedom, and discipleship?

The Determiners

In doing the rather tough work of getting a handle on fear, both our own fear and the fear burdening others, we need to sort through what makes people feel threatened or fearful. Insecurity has been defined as "deficient in assurance, beset by fear and anxiety," and "not adequately guarded or sustained." Conversely, security is a freedom from fear or anxiety, or freedom from want or deprivation. What is it that finally makes us feel either safe or threatened, assured or unassured, nurtured or enslaved?

It would seem there are three fundamental facets to living that give rise to our basic sense of Self, a Self that is either free of or beset by fear, secure or insecure. It is this sense of Self that provides the catalyst for how we respond to life. These determiners are:

the spiritual and interior life—one's relationship with God and with one's self;

the life of relationships—including family, friends, and community;

life in the social order—including *physical safety*; the meeting of *basic needs* (i.e. clean air, pure water, shelter, warmth, health care, job, housing); *cultural acceptance* rather than discrimination; and *interdependence* rather than relationships of dominance/dependence.

These three fundamental elements interact and fuse to determine who we are and how we perceive ourselves and the world around us. Ultimately, they are about love and fear, and God's will for *shalom*.[4]

The Lens of Fearfulness

It has become almost trite to describe someone as insecure. Television talk shows, magazines, and best-sellers probe our emotional insecurity, financial insecurity, and sexual insecurity *ad nauseum*. We label ourselves and each other "insecure" for manifestations as minimal as nervous laughter. Let us distance ourselves here from the casualness of the word and carefully consider the Insecure Self, in whom fear and anxiousness have first claim, a Self that is "deficient in assurance," "not adequately guarded or sustained." This is the Self that is unsure of being loved, lovable, or valued; a Self for whom the possibility of rejection is no small consideration. Self-doubt and want are daily companions, and life is awash with threatening experiences.

Fearfulness and insecurity are the basis for dealing with these experiences while self-esteem cowers. Cruel cycles of brokenness evolve that evoke defensiveness, perhaps violence, or even death. This can be a physical death or a death of the spirit; such is the great power of fear.

Every day we experience the fallout from people living in fear. Fear may even be our own condition. We are often at a loss to understand why people are so angry and defensive; why it is so difficult to relate to them. As would-be peacemakers, we are often bewildered by the barriers of hostility we encounter, not only at the global level, but within our homes, congregations, and communities. A Protestant laywoman, speaking of her assumption that people in her congregation would see peacemaking as a way to express their faith, recently said to me, "I was not prepared for the out-and-out opposition." Another had this to say: "I had no idea peacemaking could be so intense, controversial, and difficult. *How* can peacemaking be controversial?"

We who are eager to see congregations committed to the ministry of peacemaking need to discover and better understand the fears that affect people so deeply and adversely. The roots are to be found in those facets of living that give us our essence: the spiritual and interior life, the life of relationships, and life in the social order. To be alienated from God and self, estranged or isolated from others, or to experience serious conditions of adversity or injustice presents the potential for feeling "deficient in assurance and inadequately guarded or sustained." It is as if these deficiencies can write the prescription for a murky lens through which life is viewed. They are the conditions that produce fearful, defensive people and a broken, violent world.

The personal and social consequences that spin out from these cycles of insecurity and fearfulness can be observed in the chart after page 32.

2

Fear and Our Spiritual Malaise

With nations on hair-trigger nuclear alert in the name of national security, some readers may be impatient with beginning a discourse on peacemaking with an examination of the spiritual life. However, we need to consider that our nation's commitment to a first-strike policy regarding nuclear weapons did not evolve from a valueless void.[1] The policy is the extension and expression of what we as a people believe in, and of what and how we worship. I heard of a Jewish rabbi who, bewildered by the logic of the arms race, asked, "How can a people who passed judgment on Nazis at the Nuremberg Trials for transporting Jews to the ovens, now support a national commitment for taking the ovens to the people?" If you and I find such a commitment to be idolatrous, we first need to search out the defensiveness within ourselves, beginning with a spiritual search. We cannot ask the government to change that which gives expression to our collective fear without addressing the fear within our own hearts. It may be painful, but if we are to be peacemakers we must engage in spiritual examination.

Furthermore, if we want to reach those in our congregations who endorse a first-strike policy (and there are many), as well as the policy's moral underpinnings, it is necessary to delve into the spiritual aspects of peacemaking. A woman who chairs her congregation's peacemaking committee told me, "Early on, I did *not* realize the importance of peacemaking in myself. I have come to see this and work at it. I think I intended to 'lay the peacemaking on them'—another layer of ethical issues. I've learned!" The

Quakers say, "There is no *way* to peace. Rather, peace is the way."

Having said that, let's look at that first determiner that contributes to our sense of self and that gives us a grounding for responding to life: our relationship with God and with our intimate selves. We begin by considering the fears of the spirit; fears that are almost commonplace in today's experience. We see the symptoms everyday, symptoms of spiritual brokenness and spiritual poverty.

Spiritual Brokenness

Who of us has not known spiritual brokenness in which all we have believed has tumbled down around us and we have felt abandoned? We have a partner in Job: "Instead of eating, I mourn, and I can never stop groaning. Everything I fear and dread comes true. I have no peace, no rest, and my troubles never end" (Job 3:24-26). Confidence and hope become strangers as fear for today and tomorrow take hold. We dare not pray, for fear God will not answer; hanging tough alone isn't as risky as praying with expectation. At best, it's a time of terrible pain and loneliness. At worst, intimacy and sustenance may be so removed that even love for self erodes, and the ensuing despair may lead us to seek solace in withdrawing, eating, or drinking. This self-abuse, a form of violence, can be devastating to health and self-esteem, setting up cycles of brokenness within the family or on the job. In its extreme, it may lead to overt violence. As Job laments, there is no peace and the troubles never end.

Spiritual Poverty

Besides the fears that come with spiritual brokenness when it seems God is silent, we have the fears that flow from spiritual poverty when the self feels alienated from God and from the intimate self within. TV, background music, chatter, endless busyness, and lots of work provide the distractions that are needed to keep us from being *with* ourselves and *knowing* ourselves. Life may be filled with fun and success, but bereft of joy and peace. Apathy, emptiness, and hopelessness settle into a Self that has lost, or may have never known, the nourishment, forgiveness, and acceptance of a loving God.

The War Within

"The LORD is waiting to be merciful to you. He is ready to take pity on you" (Isaiah 30:18). This fearful Self is unable to trust the promise. There is too much to forgive and no proof that living could ever be any different. As guilt burrows deeper there is a longing for a Perfect Self, but the fantasy is riddled with the actual imperfections, lapses, and even voids that must be denied. Being honest with one's self borders on the impossible and our souls become layered over with self-deception. How angry and defensive we become when someone spots cracks in our self-proclaimed perfection.

Defensiveness becomes a necessity for coping with the war that wages within. The unaccepting, Imperfect Self needs enemies on whom to pin the flaws within that cannot be owned. Focusing on the inadequacies or frailties of others relieves the sense of inadequacy within. Making others feel inferior can seem to elevate our status. Self-righteous railing can be a distraction from the fear of our own moral frailties. Fault-finding and suspiciousness reveal a Self, as well as a nation, under the siege of fear.

Other signals of fear's malaise are inordinate needs to win, possess, and be recognized. Displays of power may seek to convince others that a Perfect Self is in control. In reality, the opposite is true; inside the image lives an Imperfect Self afraid of what cannot be controlled or managed.

Displays of perfection, whether in performance or appearance, may be blown to extremes to shore up self-esteem. We are surrounded by examples. I recently overheard a woman discussing the condition of her sculptured fingernails. (Sculptured nails are a commercial process for building and extending permanent, artificial nails over the natural nail.) She lamented, "By the time they repair and reshape the damaged nails it costs me $30 each visit. I don't know how much longer I can keep this up!" I wanted to ask her what would happen if she didn't. She spoke for many who burden themselves to the limit, buying those things that will give an exterior cover to that which is insecure and fearful of the humanness inside. The credit card industry has reaped the profits from our brokenness. John Kavanaugh calls it a "thingified life." Life becomes "thingified" with the thingified values of power, possessions, and pleasures.[2]

Whether we know it or not, the true inner self, which is human and imperfect, does not buy the messages of self-deception. The conflict between what is true but denied and what is false but proclaimed is like a war within. The fear of self-discovery is too painful to face. Denial extracts a toll, running the gamut from the overuse of "plastics," overwork, and alcoholism to fractured families and violence. An Episcopal priest of a suburban congregation said to me, "We live in a war zone. Everyone is involved in making war: war on ourselves, the creation, each other, and on God." Speaking of the war we make on ourselves, he said, "We have so drugged ourselves that we are not even aware of the pain in which we are living!"

The Lifestyle Connection

Beyond the effects on self and family, this spiritual malaise of fear can spiral outwards until needs for status and importance hook up with lifestyles and systems that hurt the earth and oppress others. In this country we cherish what is thought to be a right: If you can afford something you have every right to buy it and enjoy it, regardless of your state of need. "I have worked hard for my money, and I have the right to buy whatever I please with it." So goes the litany, which operates oblivious to the finiteness of the earth's resources and the needs of others.

Let me risk oversimplification with an example from the neighborhood. Recently I saw a former neighbor who had lived nearby when our children were small. Like us, their family had four children; like us, they had two bathrooms when they lived in the neighborhood (something which would have amazed my grandmother who raised five children with no running water). The family moved away and now has only two of the children living at home. She told me about their new home, mentioning its *five* bathrooms. I could scarcely contain my amazement, particularly because of my own aversion to cleaning bathrooms. "Why do you have *five* bathrooms?" I asked. She answered, "When the kids were little they always had to fight over the bathrooms" (a wonderful opportunity to learn negotiation, I thought), "so I just decided that now when they come home they can each have their own bathroom!" One is left to wonder about the guilt and status needs that fuel such a decision. Furthermore, this is an example of how these excesses create a national shopping list for minerals and precious metals that finally makes nuclear weapons "important to protect our national interest." It reflects why U.S. business interests in South Africa, with its chrome, magnesium, and other scarce natural resources, preclude a stronger rejection of apartheid by our government.

Our spiritual nature as individuals and families takes on a new reality with the way we spend or don't spend our money. While the connection may seem obscure when we pay our bills each month, our checkbooks and the lifestyle they represent are at one end of a connection that fans out to just and unjust systems and governments all over the world. There is a connection between our spiritual needs, our values, and our lifestyles.

It is as if lifestyle and spirituality gave off soundings to each other. The drive for status, power, and importance by our nonaccepting, Imperfect Selves can provide the link to fear's systemic violence. Fear's spiritual poverty can produce a people whose need to feel superior and powerful fuels the systems of racism, sexism, elitism, and war making. It is at this point that the spiritual poverty of some contributes to the material poverty of others; it is here that the spiritual fears of the few spawn fears for survival for the many. Fear's harvest is more fear for those suffering under the social and economic injustice of these practices; needs and wounds have become intertwined. Indeed, fear becomes the power of nothingness where there is no hope, no *shalom*. It is, as Wallis said, faith's final contradiction. (See chart after page 32.)

Does this not tell us why the very words "peace and justice" seem to come down so hard on many mainline Christian congregations? We are a people afraid. Christian peacemaking, apart from spiritual conversion, is like a plant cutting without roots. It might spruce up a drab corner for a short time, but it will wither when the sun gets hot and the climate is less than ideal. At the time when its shade is sorely needed, it is no more. For our peacemaking to take root and offer shade, we must first abandon our fear and believe in the promises of the faith.

"Do Not Be Afraid, I Am with You"

"Israel, the LORD who created you says; 'Do not be afraid—I will save you. I have called you by name—you are mine. When you pass through deep waters, I will be with you; your troubles will not overwhelm you. . . . For I am the LORD your God. . . . I love you and give you honor. Do not be afraid—I am with you!' " (Isaiah 43:1, 2, 4, 5).

The Scriptures are rich in testimonies speaking of God's yearning for us to receive the gift of God's perfect love, so that all fear might be put to rest. "Do not be afraid—I am with you," God said to ancient Israel. "I love you and give you honor." Years later, God's covenant of love broke into history in a new way in Jesus. "For this is how God loved the world: he gave his only Son, so that everyone who believes in him may not perish but have eternal life. For God sent his Son into the world not to judge the world, but so that through him the world might be saved" (John 3:16-17. NJB). God, the author of peace, has given the world and all people for all time the gift of peace through the redeeming death and resurrection of God's own son, Jesus. Christ Jesus has come to live in us (John 15). *Take this to heart: We are loved, cherished, and forgiven; we are totally accepted. God offers us peace.*

God has accepted that in our lives which we cannot accept and have denied—that which we have exhausted ourselves to forget through amassing things, status, power, and recognition. God's loving and valuing of us runs so deep that, if we will but "open the door," Christ will come into our house and eat with us (Revelation 3:20). We can receive the gift of grace and even begin to love and accept ourselves.

We can be freed from our preoccupation with defensiveness and self-deception; we no longer need to pretend, defend, or try to forget who we are, for we belong to God!

Claimed and Healed

When we know who we are and to whom we belong, we can be liberated from a culture that works like a predator on our guilt and insecurities. We will no longer need the biggest, the best, the newest, and the most or be the highest, brightest, and most acknowledged to prove to ourselves that we are lovable and valuable. We will not have to live in fear of imagined enemies. "I love you and honor you" Yahweh says. Within our intimate selves we will know God values us; we can then love and honor ourselves. We will be at peace.

Through God's claim on us, as little children held close, we are assured and sustained. We are secure, belonging not to Caesar, but to God. Our hearts can be disarmed and healed. We can say no to Caesar's intimidation, entrenchment, and violence; we can say yes to God's invitation to newness, hope, and even vulnerability. Where our spiritual poverty once spawned suffering for ourselves and others, we now feel the healing power of spiritual conversion as we are called to new possibilities. Through God's transforming love, we are invited

— to be spiritually renewed,
— to witness to God's love in our relationships,
— to be open to the pain of others, especially the weak and the poor,
— to live lives of nonviolence and justice through deeds of solidarity and suffering love.

This is peacemaking. It is a response to God's peacegiving.

Hear the Good News: "When anyone is joined to Christ, he is a new being; the old is gone, the new has come. All this is done by God, who through Christ changed us from enemies into his friends and gave us the task of making others his friends also" (2 Corinthians 5:17-18).

3

The Need to Be Loved and to Belong

"These three remain: faith, hope, and love; and the greatest of these is love" (1 Corinthians 13:13).

"No one has ever seen God, but if we love one another, God lives in union with us, and his love is made perfect in us" (1 John 4:12).

Love is essential to the life of *shalom*. For proof, some would quote Corinthians: "the greatest of these is love." Some would quote psychologists such as Abraham Maslow, whose research found love and belongingness to be among the basic human needs. Some would not need to quote anyone but would reflect in their own lives the security of a loving family, good friends, and a caring community.

Having others present to us in our joys and sorrows, successes and disappointments, pain and confusion is to have God's love made real. Loving relationships provide balm for healing fear's wounds and restoring shaken confidence and esteem. A loving home, where affirmation, acceptance, and openness are part of the daily diet is a refuge that nurtures secure children who will later not need imagined enemies on which to project Disowned Selves.[1] Intimacy, honesty, sharing, cooperation, and positive resolution of conflicts are but a few of the ways that we come to know love's security through our relationships.

Unloved and Disconnected

The need to be loved and to belong is a need that goes unmet with frightening frequency. Pastors, juvenile officers, therapists, and bartenders have daily experiences in dealing with vast numbers of people who suffer loneliness, rejection, isolation, and estrangement. The condition does not respect age, race, or economic status; it is to be found in nursing homes, holdover cells, affluent condominiums, and unheated flats. People who have been ignored, forgotten, or abused are within our sight, if not our consciousness, every day.

We see some of the desperate consequences of broken relationships and lonely lives reported regularly in the media. Recently the *St. Louis Post-Dispatch* quoted a police officer's comment on a violent encounter, which included murder, between two rival street gangs: "They are a group of youngsters who came together for survival and identity. It's negative energy, but that is the purpose of it."[2]

Beyond the spectacular examples of persons with unmet needs for love and belonging are the countless in our midst who, day in and day out, want for the security of a loving family, intimate friends, or caring community—people who, for whatever reason, do not feel connected. The "others" in their lives may be dead, too busy with "important things," never home, alcoholic, or incapable of giving love themselves. The result can be a Self who feels unloved, and perhaps unlovable or unworthy of being loved and valued. Feelings of anxiousness and uncertainty, rather than love and acceptance, become the basis for responding to life. Anger, guilt, jealousy, inadequacy, and hurt become part of this legacy of the fear of not being loved.

As we have seen, fearfulness sets up destructive cycles of brokenness. Here we consider the fear born of inadequate relationships. On its milder side it is the Self who is very uncomfortable with herself or himself and ill at ease with others. In its extremes, it is the Self who has been denied the basic human need of love, intimacy, and belongingness, who responds to the world in angry and violent ways that seem less than human. Violent and bizarre behavior that explodes upon others can be at the end of the line: *The insecurity of one finally affects the security of others. All are ultimately diminished.* It is as if spiritual poverty has bred a poverty in relationships, making a cycle of brokenness. Here again, fear has become the contradiction of God's will for *shalom*.

Developing the Capacity for Justice

Developmental psychologists have studied the connection between the denial of love and human moral development. The work of Abraham Maslow, who died in 1970, provides us with another way for understanding what we have called personal outcomes to fear that renew the cycles of brokenness. Maslow identified a growth process consisting of a series of stages through which people pass in developing their fullest human potential. He found that the stages of human development correspond with the satisfying of certain Basic Needs. The Basic Needs begin with the body's needs for air, water, and food. They are followed by safety needs and *needs for belonging, love, respect, and self-esteem*. From that point in the progression of needs and development, Maslow found that people move from Basic Needs to Meta or Being Needs in which they develop the capacity for knowledge, beauty, truth, wholeness, justice, peace, universal love, harmony, etc. According to Maslow's theory, the Basic Needs must be reasonably met before the Being Needs and potential can evolve. Unmet needs, whether at the Basic level or at the Being level result in an "illness of deprivation" (spiritual, psychological, and/or physical) that plays out in negative behavior.[3]

Maslow's theory has tremendous implications for world peace. To restate, Maslow found people cannot move on to the Being Needs, where the capacity for truth, justice, peace, harmony, and universal love is realized until the Basic Needs are reasonably met, which includes the needs to feel safe, be loved, and have a sense of belonging.

It is vital to mentally underscore the place that *belongingness and love* have in basic human needs when approaching the work of peace and justice in the congregation. Many in the religious peace movement strongly identify with Pope Paul VI's adaptation of Isaiah 32:16: "If you want peace, work for justice." It would seem to be so elementary as to be beyond question. Not so! Over and over when dealing with our congregations we hit the brick wall of fear and hostility when the peace and justice issues are raised. Addressing issues like the arms race, sanctuary, and welfare reform is often *verboten*.

This would seem to suggest a corollary to "If you want peace, work for justice." It is: "If you want people to work for justice, remember they need to be loved." I have seen ersatz peacemaking that could never change hearts because the law of love was forgotten. Henri Nouwen has commented on this:

> Words of peace have often been used cheaply by those whose root preoccupation was to be victorious. Peacemaking is a work of love and love casts out fear. Nothing is more important in peacemaking than that it flows from a deep and undeniable experience of love. Only those who know they are loved and rejoice in that love can be true peacemakers, because the intimate knowledge of being loved sets us free to look beyond the boundaries of death and to speak and act fearlessly for peace.[4]

Living the Good News

In a helpful booklet, *Pastoring for Peace and Justice*, Alfred Krass lays out some rules for prophets: "When all is said and done, what we say from the pulpit or in a class only goes as far as our own actions. A desire to change people is not a legitimate reason for being in ministry. If, however, you minister to people on a regular basis, they'll give second thought to rejecting your controversial opinions out of hand." Krass recalls hearing of a man who was astounded to see a "reactionary" neighbor taking part in a welfare-rights demonstration on the steps of the state capitol. "What on earth are you doing here?" he asked his neighbor. "Rev. Yordon asked me to come," the neighbor explained. "Anybody who ministered to me the way Hank did when I was sick in the hospital, I listen to."[5]

The needs for love and belonging are basic to *everyone*—even to those we sometimes make the mistake of labeling. It is a blessing God hasn't labeled us. Instead, God has *claimed* us, just as God has claimed those whom we sometimes find it hard to love. When it comes to loving enemies who are the everyday variety and who seem to sow land mines among our efforts for justice, loving can be done in the very concrete manner of according to them the human dignity that God has willed for each of us.

I recently asked some people involved in peacemaking in their congregations, "What lessons have you learned from mistakes and disappointments?" A woman who chairs the peace task force of her church responded, "I am constantly learning more about reconciliation and I need to learn much more. I think this is the case for the whole of the congregation. And it is so difficult!"

Christ's life, death, and resurrection tell us of God's sovereign intention for the reconciliation of all creation with itself and with God. We are loved and we belong. Have we allowed ourselves to receive this gift? Do we act on it with those close at hand?

"I give you a new commandment: love one another. As I have loved you, so must you love one another" (John 13:34).

4

When Insecurity Becomes an Institution

We began our examination of the things that make people fearful by defining insecurity as: "deficient in assurance, beset by fears and anxiety, not adequately guarded or sustained." In considering the fears of the Insecure Self, we must come to terms with the insecurity born of injustice. To do this, let us clarify what we mean by justice.

In his book *Bread and Justice*, James McGinnis notes that "in simple terms, justice has long been understood as giving each person his or her due. And what is due . . . is the fundamental right to live a fully human life."[1] McGinnis describes the components of justice that nurture a fully human life. Each component is rooted in the stages of human development and in the Christian understanding of human dignity. He identifies them as: *sufficient life goods* or economic rights; *dignity/esteem* or cultural rights; *participation* or political rights; and *solidarity* or the responsibility to assure these rights with and for others. His schema, which is helpful to our understanding of fear, looks like this:[2] (See chart on page 32.)

The Injustice of the National Security State

In considering the fear and insecurity born of injustice, we begin with a violation of justice that is visited upon every person in the world by the nuclear arms race. The nuclear arms race is a

Components of Justice	Their Christian Basis	Stages of Human Development
SUFFICIENT LIFE-GOODS—food, shelter, clothing, health care, skills development, work (economic rights)	The earth is the Lord's; it is for the use of all; stewardship	Security (concern for survival)
DIGNITY/ESTEEM — recognizing, affirming & calling forth the value/ uniqueness of each person and each people (cultural rights)	Each person is created in the image and likeness of God	Self-worth (concern for personal recognition)
PARTICIPATION — the right of individuals & peoples to shape their own destinies (political rights)	Each person is called by Jesus to help build His Kingdom in our world	Self-determination (concern for control over one's life)
SOLIDARITY—the corresponding duty to promote these rights with & for others (duties as well as rights)	We are created in the image of a God Who is a (community) Trinity of persons	Interdependence (concern for others)

violation of the component of *participation*, which assures people the right to shape their own destiny through political involvement. Today humanity does not enjoy the collective assurance of a viable destiny; the lives of people are at the mercy of the very few who determine the nature for resolving conflicts of national interest. This is the injustice of the national security state, a term with global application.

Robert McAfee Brown, in discussing the response of the church to the national security state, notes that "In the national security state, the normal situation . . . is one of 'emergency' in which the appropriate doctrine is: Anything goes." He says that in one of the most important insights from the meeting of the Roman Catholic bishops in Puebla, Mexico in 1979,

> The bishops noted that when the state "presents itself as an Absolute holding sway over persons, in its name *the insecurity of the individual becomes institutionalized*". . . . [The]

doctrine is really an ideology . . . which demands uncritical acceptance and the delegation of power to a minority that "suppresses the broad-based participation of the people in political decisions. . . . It puts the people under the tutelage of military and political elites . . . and it leads to increased inequality."[3]

Beyond jeopardizing the existence of the earth and denying participation in the decisions of true security, the economics of the nuclear arms race violates the component of *sufficient life goods*. The costs are nearly incomprehensible and they take away food, shelter, health care, and even jobs from people all over the world.[4] It would be no exaggeration to say that people are dying from national security. Perhaps we should say they are dying from the institutionalized insecurity of national security. The arms race is a source of fear; it is unjust, and it affects us all.

Gerald and Patricia Mische point out that the frustration of human needs and the low priority given to other important human values because of "the national security straitjacket" have resulted "in a sense of emptiness, incompletion, and alienation. . . . There is a strong relationship between the social and human deterioration (drug addiction, alcoholism, materialism) so widespread today and the deprivation of meaning and other human needs suffered in a system dominated by the security imperative."[5] Once again we see the fruits of fear's sad harvest.

Fear and Structures That Do Violence

Beyond the arms race are other insecurities born of other injustices that peacemakers must consider if we are to have a handle on fear. As one who does not have to make a choice between heating and eating, and as one who can sleep without fear of husband or children being carried away by the police as we sleep, it is impossible for me to presume to know firsthand the feelings of the oppressed. One must read, listen, observe. Better yet, through solidarity efforts, one can stand with the oppressed and be affected by their unending struggles to simply *be*.

In situations where the structures are violent in their injustice and where solidarity is absent, fear's pain is etched on the faces of those who suffer. The dazed look of Vera, a homeless woman with a green blanket who took refuge in our office building last winter, revealed the look of fear's emptiness. The eyes of black South Africans burying murdered victims of apartheid reveal unspeakable grief. Violent outcomes of recent farm foreclosures are voices of fear's desperation. These are lives "deficient in assurance," inadequately sustained.

Grinding poverty, assaults on human rights, and policies or systems that deny people dignity are heavy messages for the Self to receive. The elimination of a job, diminished health services, denial of the need for decent day care, or inadequate public housing say to people, "You are not valued." "You are disposable." "We reject the likes of you." To preach pride and self-respect to those whose value and dignity go unacknowledged by society is futile, for the potential for self-loathing is built right into the system. This wretched slice of insecurity breeds feelings of being unheard, excluded, and cheated. Outrageous behavior should come as no surprise when there is nothing to be lost. Overt acts of violence, whether they are the everyday street variety or acts of terrorism and revolution, provide the mirror for fear's systemic violence.

Martin Luther King, Jr. sought to teach us about this:

> We are all caught in an inescapable network of mutuality, tied into a single garment of destiny. Whatever affects one directly, affects all indirectly. We are made to live together because of the interrelated structure of reality. . . . We aren't going to have peace on earth until we recognize this basic fact.[6]

Miracles and the Law of Love

"I have come in order that you might have life—life in all its fullness" (John 10:10).

Jesus' life and ministry were an expression of God's will for *shalom*, for life in a fullness of equity, harmony, and community. Justice is the condition of his message of love and reconciliation, for he proclaimed "Good News to the afflicted . . . liberty to captives, sight to the blind, [and] let the oppressed go free" (Luke 4:18, NJB).

Theologian Douglas Meeks once said that miracles are what happen when God's justice and righteousness are present.[7] Our nation and world are in need of new miracles. We, who have suffered the afflictions of our own guilt and spiritual fears, have been given the Good News of God's power for life. We are called to be bringers of the miracles, to bring the nature of God's righteousness to the structures of injustice. Yahweh told the community of ancient Israel, "Love your neighbor as you love yourself" (Leviticus 19:18). Centuries later, Jesus said to his disciples, "My commandment is this: love one another, just as I love you" (John 15:12). How should Christians respond to this today in the public arena? Elaine Saum writes, "Politics is love in action. It is the inevitable means by which we as individuals and as groups love our neighbors. To love our neighbors is to work toward a time *when the law of love coincides with the law of the land.*" [emphasis added][8]

The community that accords dignity through health care, education, jobs, housing, and voting rights for all is making love tangible in its public policy. The nation that accords security through economic and social justice, respect for international law and interdependence, and nonviolent ways of resolving conflicts of national interest is a nation seeking to make the law of love coincide with the law of the land.

Justice, dignity, and liberty for all people is the stuff of miracles. We whom God has loved, forgiven, and accepted have been charged to be agents of those miracles. The halls of Congress, the state capitol, city hall, and the local hearing are arenas for bringing love's law of justice and compassion to fruition in public law and policy. Let us be about God's business!

In Conclusion

There are three fundamental facets to living that determine our sense of self; they are the spiritual or interior life, the life of relationships, and life in the social order. Within these determiners are conditions that form a Self that is either secure or insecure, free of fear or beset by it, defensive or open. The conditions are those of spiritual wholeness or spiritual poverty; love and community, or estrangement and isolation; equitable living conditions or conditions of injustice. It is the resulting sense of Self that provides the base for how we respond to life. One is a base grounded in fear; the other, in the certainty of being loved and valued.

The bottom line is that the Self either experiences the knowledge of being loved, valued, and sustained or the Self feels threatened, fearful, anxious, and powerless. The Insecure Self, having a sense of being unloved, unlovable, or perhaps rejected, is likely to be unaccepting of itself and threatened by others. Defensiveness becomes necessary to cope with the ensuing sense of powerlessness. Brokenness and violence can follow.

Because of the relationship of fear, defensiveness, and violence to the spiritual life, the life of relationships, and the social order, these determiners need to be carefully considered in the ministry of peacemaking. An understanding of the nature of peacemaking begins to take form. It points to the need to address the reasons and conditions of fearfulness, so that people and nations alike might know the security found in being loved, valued, accepted, and respected.

When we look at the attitudes and feelings that go hand-in-hand with fear, and when we consider the behavior that flows from it, it doesn't take long to discover how fearful we actually are—we who would be peacemakers. It is vital that we comprehend the close-knit relationship between spiritual wholeness and peacemaking. While spiritual poverty in some contributes to material poverty and institutional violence for many others, our own spiritual transformation can be the starting place for breaking fear's cycles of brokenness. Disarming the heart is where it begins. We can be healed; freed to love ourselves as well as others. With that miracle, others can follow.

Part II

Moving from Fear to Love

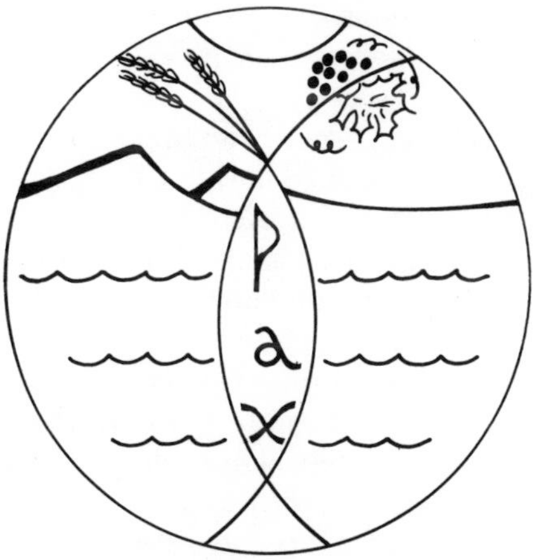

5

Called to Peacemaking

"God is love, and whoever lives in love lives in union with God and God lives in union with him. . . . There is no fear in love; perfect love drives out all fear" (1 John 4:16, 18).

When we reflect upon our fears, who cares to admit how many of them have had to do with wanting to be liked, loved, or accepted by others because of our own self-doubts? Will they like me? Will they approve? Have I made them angry? How many of our fears have had to do with rejection or with our own self-imposed burden of the Perfect Self, a burden made heavier by the false roles and destructive habits we have created to maintain that illusion? Through God's gift of peace in Jesus, God says to us, "Fear not. You are loved; you are forgiven and accepted. Be at peace!" Secure in this blessing of grace, fears begin to lose their claim, and masks can finally drop. Peacemaking can then begin!

As a response to God's peacegiving, peacemaking says yes to God's power of life, yes to God's righteousness. In this act of faith we move out of the cycles of fear and brokenness and into what Henri Nouwen calls the House of Love, referring to John 14: 23.[1] "Anyone who loves me will keep my word, and my Father will love him, and we shall come to him and make a home in him" (NJB). When we receive God's gift of grace we receive the certainty of being fully loved and valued. We can then honestly acknowledge our own needfulness and incompleteness. Self-acceptance begins to take seed and we can even begin to love ourselves. Blessed with God's assurance we are finally secure.

When you consider how many marketing schemes depend upon the fears of rejection and insecurity, it is not difficult to imagine how receiving this gift of grace and acceptance can bring joy and balance into our lifestyle and spending habits. We can be freed to be just, to live more simply and compassionately. Our spiritual *metanoia*, or turning around, can be the starting place for a new dynamic in which our habits, talents, and gifts intersect with doing the work of justice.

Peacemaking and Prayer

Prayer provides the vessel for moving from the cycles of fear to the House of Love. It is in prayer that we reclaim our true identity and purpose. We recall that before we were claimed by the culture, the nation, or the world, we were claimed by God; it is God to whom we belong, not Caesar. It is in God that we find our true security; not in the false idols of a "thingified" and armed existence.[2] Wallis puts it this way: "Prayer, while offered for the sake of the world, will change those who pray . . . . Prayer humbles us. It starts in confession and repentance and recalls our identity as God's people. To pray is to recognize that, before the evil can be overcome, we must be transformed."[3]

John Kavanaugh calls prayer a life task, a commitment in which we disengage ourselves from the demands of the culture and in which we risk placing faith and hope in another. Kavanaugh's discussion of the moments of prayer is helpful and to the point. He says that moments of prayer are:

— a freely entered presence to ourselves, to our deepest longings, and to the personal God we profess to believe in—involving, at the first step, acts of faith, hope, and *acceptance of ourselves as we are*;

— a recognition and truthful acceptance of our poverty and needfulness in the presence of God, and a crying out from our human frailty;

— a listening to God's response (such a listening is possible only when we accept our own incompleteness) not only in

Scripture but also in the moments within ourselves; and

— a giving of thanks and returning of ourselves to God when we recognize that we are loved into being and loved for our very being.[4]

In returning ourselves to God, we experience reality in the promise: "Do not be afraid; I am with you"; and in this new security of love we can begin to transcend ourselves. Receiving God's gift of peace opens new possibilities for hope and vulnerability, for when we live with a knowledge of Christ's presence within us, we can begin to see Christ in others as well. We can begin to see Christ present in the lives of the suffering, the poor, and the oppressed, and we feel called to respond. As we find ways to enter into their pain, the sense of suffering love begins to take root, and we are called to peacemaking.

The Call to Peacemaking

Peacemaking is a ministry of hope, a work of love. God calls us to intervene in the world's cycles of brokenness and violence by changing the conditions that make people fearful and defensive. We are needed to help dismantle the vast web of fear that spins out from spiritual poverty and personal estrangement to unjust systems and nuclear weapons. The task before us is to nurture authentic security. Our job description reads: deeds of suffering love, justice, and reconciliation. We have Christ's assurance that we will not be alone in the certain struggle. As peacemakers we will seek to honor God's reign through spiritual wholeness and caring relationships, working for a nation of justice and a world at peace. When hearts are disarmed, swords can be made into plowshares and God's will for shalom *comes into its fullness.*

The hope of peacemaking is not to be confused with naive optimism; it is an intentional way of living that brings love and risk to the cycles of brokenness. Moltmann states that "those who hope in Christ can no longer put up with reality as it is, but begin to suffer under it, and to contradict it."[5] St. Augustine put it another way. He said that Hope has two daughters, Anger and Courage: Anger that things are not what they ought to be, and

Courage to make them what they must be.[6] This is the hope of the peacemaker.

Called to Be as Well as to Do

In the spiritual journey of disarming the heart, the word "seek" is of significance. "Seek" provides the bridge between who we are called to be and who we are now. "Seek" states with honesty the tension that exists between the call and the track record. We seek to be agents of hope; we find ourselves at times despairing. We seek to live securely in the House of Love, but we find ourselves fearful and defensive. We talk about openness but are sometimes strident with those who don't see life in the way we do. We pass resolutions about resisting policies of injustice and we are afraid to declare sanctuary. We pray for peace and pay taxes for war. We seek to see Christ in others, but too often feel threatened by everyday enemies of our own making—those on whom we project our own shadows of fear. We live lives of contradiction.

It is as if we have divorced the Being and Doing facets of our very nature. We are searching out things to do for peace and justice, while we have forgotten who we are: children loved, forgiven, accepted, and claimed by God. Splitting our Doing from our Being is in itself a source of brokenness, a form of violence we inflict upon ourselves. *Shalom* has to do with wholeness where the Doing and the Being sides of our nature are in harmony. As peacemakers, then, we must consider who we seek to *be* as well as what we are to *do*. We know we are called to respond to God's peacegiving with peacemaking and justice-seeking. What will be our nature?

To live out of the security of God's graciousness is to be freed to say Yes to life. Fear's defensiveness is tranformed into love's vulnerability. In Micah the question is asked, "What does the Lord require?" The answer comes, "to do what is just, to show constant love, and to live in humble fellowship with our God" (Micah 6:8). Repentance and thanksgiving create the context for this humble fellowship. From the repentant and thankful spirit grows a self that is no longer afraid. Shrinking not from introspection and reclaiming its own shadows, it is a self that can then be fully open and freed, strong enough to be vulnerable.

Vulnerability is on the Being side of peacemaking. It is recognized by openness, for it is vested in a basic human truth: As members of God's family, we are fundamentally one. Differences are valued. That which is new, foreign, or different is not automatically feared, whether it be a person, an issue or ideology, or a culture. Vulnerability listens and trusts, not only others but itself.

Hand-in-hand with vulnerability, we are called to truthfulness. To one who is grounded in love rather than fear, truth will not pose a threat, and peacemaking requires that we try to discern the truth for our times. It is rarely an easy task. Listening to people with experiences different from our own, learning from the victims of injustice, reading from a wide range of sources, and reflecting on the times in the scriptural context of God's will for justice and reconciliation are part of the search for truth.

Speaking the truth, and speaking it in love, is yet another way that the power of fear is dispelled. Speaking honestly and openly with others about differences in a way that both truthfulness and relationships are valued gives integrity to peacemaking. Rhetoric, careless labeling, and inflammatory language for its own sake, especially when done under the guise of peace and justice, do not contribute to resolving or reconciling differences. When they are used, fear rather than love is probably speaking.

Finally, the essence of the Being side of Christian peacemaking will be found in living in community. William Gibson observes "Community is the arena of mutual love—intrinsic to *shalom*, essential to human fulfillment. The solidarity of love requires community in which all participate as full and equal members."[7] Community has roots in God's covenant with Israel, it was made new in the life and ministry of Christ, it found vibrant expression in the early church, and is today in a constant state of renewal and regeneration. Gibson notes that "the configurations of persons from which a sense of community may emerge are countless—from the intimate face to face communities that support us day by day to the all-inclusive 'global community.'" Family and congregation are two immediate circles where community can be lived and experienced.

"Community means people in solidarity with each other: affirming, trusting, supporting, enjoying each other, and engaging together in common endeavor."[8] Whether it be a family, a congregation, a work group, or a religious order, the community that is grounded in God's will for justice and righteousness will extend the qualities of community beyond itself.

The solidarity of love will call the community of justice to identify with the poor and the powerless in deeds of hope and righteous anger. Rev. Allan Boesak, a courageous anti-apartheid activitist in South Africa, calls it a holy rage. He speaks of

> the ability to rage when justice lies prostrate on the streets and when the lie rages across the face of the earth. A holy anger about things that are wrong in the world. To rage against the ravaging of God's earth and the destruction of God's world. To rage at the senseless killing of so many and against the madness of militarism. To rage at the lie that calls the threat of death and the strategy of destruction 'peace', to rage against the complacency of so many in the church who fail to see that we shall live only by the truth, and that our fear will be the death of us all.[9]

Righteous anger affirms God's will for community in deeds of compassion and in the willingness to get at root causes of suffering.

A Harmony in Being and Doing

We have looked very briefly at the Being side of peacemaking: repentance, thanksgiving, vulnerability, truthfulness, and community with the capacity for mutuality, compassion, courage, and righteous anger. Let us now look at the Doing side to which these Being qualities are wedded. When hearts have been disarmed and when there is harmony within, Doing will flow from Being and peacemaking will challenge the cycles of fear. What might be some of the marks of a life so unified? The list that follows is not complete, but rather will engage the reader in further reflection.

LOVE'S CALL TO BEING	LOVE'S CALL TO DOING
Repentant	Forgiving, reconciling
Thankful and joyful	Confessing God's grace and *shalom* Faithful use of talents and gifts Intimacy with friends Appreciating the earth Playful, able to laugh
Introspective	Comfortable with silence Open to oneself Faithful in prayer and meditation
Vulnerable	Open to newness and differences Listening Trusting Open to new facts and information Open to risk Open to pain
Truthful	Seeking out varied sources of information Open to evaluation Discerning of good and evil Assertive Learning and using good communication skills
Interdependent	Nurturing community and mutuality Sharing and conserving Caring, affirming and supporting Seeking to cooperate rather than compete Leadership: collaborative instead of hierarchical; sharing power In conflict or confrontation: firm but not aggressive, using skills in nonviolent conflict resolution

Courageous	Unafraid to be different from the culture or peers Confident Acting with moral integrity Creative in problem solving Tenacious Consistent Not easily intimidated; grounded in vulnerability rather than defensiveness
Compassionate	Letting in the pain of others Knowing and naming the poor and those who suffer
Righteously angry and hopeful	Acting in solidarity with the earth and with people who are victims of fear's systemic consequences through: prayer, deeds of mercy, legislative action, advocacy and organizing, public protest, active nonviolence, sacrificial action (e.g. fasting)

We have all felt the shortfall of love in our lives, for we have suffered with the inconsistencies between despair and hope, defensiveness and vulnerability, chaos and peace. By abandoning fear and trusting in the promises of God we can come into wholeness where Being and Doing finally are one. This journey of the heart can then go outward, helping to arrest the cycles of fear in a broken world.

"There is no fear in love; perfect love drives out all fear" (1 John 4:18).

6

Peacemaking and Our Daily Relationships

In the Vietnam War years of the early 70s, our three daughters were in various stages of adolescence. It may be remembered how youth latched onto the symbols and semantics of those who protested the war. The words "love" and "peace" were to be found everywhere, along with flowers and peace symbols. In our household they were on the girls' notebooks, bulletin boards, tee shirts, and any other available surface. However, despite the abundance of the words "love" and "peace," there were the usual household arguments about staying in the shower too long, playing stereos too loud, and other typical grievances of siblings in the early teen years. Finally, one day in frustration over the contradictions of my budding "peaceniks," I made a sign for the refrigerator that read, "LOVE your sister! PEACE in the kitchen!" Predictably, the sign was greeted with rolling eyes and long-suffering sighs, but the point was made that if you are to be credible about your concern for love and peace, you need to be consistent.

Consistent are the peacemakers! Or at least we need to seek very hard to be consistent. How we treat people in the every day of life says volumes about our peacemaking. Self-proclaimed peacemakers tend to be action-oriented folks, and therein lies a danger: the peril that we may be so committed to achieving results that we don't hear or are insensitive to the needs of those immediately around us. Our integrity is in jeopardy if we dismiss, with calloused feelings and preoccupied minds, those with whom we live, work, and worship while we "work for world peace." Our egos and needs for control will provide the litmus test for self-examination. Living out of love means we will respect and value the people with whom we rub shoulders daily: our family, the people in the workplace, the people who provide us with services, the checker in the market, and the fellow in the next lane of traffic. Those near to us will be treated with kindness and consideration.

Peacemaking has to do with making God's love real in the relationships of family, friends, and community. It is here that the basic needs to be loved and to belong are either met or go unnourished. Peacemakers will seek to create environments of security, warmth, and cooperation in our homes, schools, and congregations where relationships with each other can teach us about the nature of a loving God.

As peacemakers we will nurture our children with toys and books that teach cooperation and compassion, rather than war-making and exploitation. Television's lessons of violence, casual sex, stereotypes, and materialism will be countered by modeling the alternatives within the crucible of the family and congregations. Parenting for peace and justice will be intentional.[1]

The security of a disarmed heart will be reflected in the way we handle power. In our dealings with each other, competing will give way to collaborating, and the need for controlling others will diminish. We will discover that winners and losers aren't the only possible outcome in resolving differences. Force and intimidation will lose their attraction when the skills of nonviolent conflict management enable us to negotiate agreement amicably for mutual gain. Reconciliation can then become more than a word from Scripture.

There is a dimension to peacemaking that calls us to go against the norm of what is comfortable or popular, whether it be in the home, congregation, or community. The further apart we are in ideology from those around us, the more difficult this can be. This can present a difficult tension of deciding when to operate within the present situation, seeking to find ways to bring about a new understanding, and when to proceed unsupported with the attending risks. Differing opinions in such areas as lifestyle, patriotism, and public protest can be difficult to deal with in the family as well as the congregation. In discerning which is the faithful alternative, one might consider: Is my ego or my own defensiveness getting in the way of a faithful choice? Is my own insecurity determining my choice? Am I responding out of love or fear? Which alternative will be most meaningful in intervening in fear's cycles of brokenness? How might I respond to the fears of the people affected by my decision?

Friendship

What else will the call to peacemaking mean in our relationships with others? We are called to friendship, to being present to others in the day-to-day, especially those who are sick, grieving, or those who are lonely for whatever reason. To be lonely and cut off from others can evoke the fears of being unaccepted and unvalued. Staying on top of this friendship intention is a challenge in today's relentless pace of obligations and responsibilities. If we return to the thought of seeing Christ in others, we might rethink priorities and at the very least have notes, greeting cards, and phone calls as part of the weekly routine.

The flip side of being present to others is allowing others to be present to us. Receiving can be difficult for some people. This is a loss because receiving the affection of others is yet another way of letting God's *shalom* into our lives. Touching, affirming, laughing, and crying with those with whom we feel safe in intimacy allows us the gift of feeling secure and sustained, and it lessens our need for defensiveness. The mistake we often make is to be so braced for the job, the schedule, and the threats that we perceive to be real, that we miss the opportunities for giving and receiving friendship that are daily within our reach. When we do this, we deny ourselves needed sustenance.

Everyday Enemies

We also need to consider the enemies of our daily existence: people who are difficult and hurtful, persons who have wronged us, or those with whom we have strong differences. Dr. Diane Perlman has done some remarkable work in *Humanizing the Enemy and Ourselves*.[2] In the exercise "Enemy Imaging in Everyday Life," Perlman poses questions about our everyday enemies, asking us to think about someone with whom we are in conflict or whom we dislike, suggesting a boss, co-worker, relative, ex-spouse, or political figure.

Among the questions Perlman asks are: How much energy do

you invest in putting this person down? How much do you enjoy getting agreement from your allies about how bad he/she is? To what extent does putting this person down make you feel good about yourself? How uncomfortable do you feel if you get information about this person that contradicts your theory about him/her? How reluctant are you to change your opinion and let go of your dislike? What would you be giving up?

Dr. Perlman's questions force us to examine our grounding and insecurities. Are we grounded in fear or love? I am reminded of some wise words of counsel my father gave me years ago. He said "Honey, it is impossible to like everyone, but always try to love everyone."

In the Sermon on the Mount, Christ taught, "Love your enemies and pray for those who persecute you. . . . If you save your greetings for your brothers, are you doing anything exceptional? . . . You must therefore set no bounds to your love, just as your heavenly Father sets none to his" (Matthew 5:43-48, NJB). How to respond to those who consistently wrong us? Wallis' statement that prayer will change those who pray has application here. Might our prayer be that we find the faithfulness to see Christ in that person and, responding out of love rather than some slice of fear or insecurity, that we maintain an openness that allows for the possibility for the other's defensiveness and hostility to finally lessen? If we can somehow remain in the House of Love in our attitudes, feelings, and behavior, we nurture the possibility for our enemy to perhaps find the space to be open to reconciliation and friendship.

There are times, however, when we meet with failure in achieving reconciliation because the power of relationship rests in *both* people. Loving requires a freedom on both sides; those we love have the freedom to withdraw. Sometimes the most loving thing we can do is to allow that without letting it diminish our own sense of worth. If we can accept this without returning hurt for hurt, we can attain glimpses of God's nature of forgiveness.

In India the word "*Namasté*" is spoken as a greeting and a farewell. The spirit of *Namasté* is the spirit of loving relationships. It means, "I honor the place in you where the universe resides; I honor the place in you of love, of light, of truth, of Peace. I honor the place within you where, if you are in that place in you and I am in that place in me, there is only one of us. *Namasté*."[3] So be it in our relationships!

7

Reordering Our Lives

"The Sovereign LORD said, 'You have sinned too long, you rulers of Israel! Stop your violence and oppression. Do what is right and just. You must never again drive my people off their land. I, the Sovereign LORD, am telling you this'" (Ezekiel 45:9).

"The LORD has told us what is good. What he requires of us is this: to do what is just, to show constant love, and to live in humble fellowship with our God" (Micah 6:8).

"[Jesus] stood up to read, and they handed him the scroll of the Prophet Isaiah. Unrolling the scroll he found the place where it is written:

The Spirit of the Lord is on me,
for he has anointed me
to bring the good news to the afflicted.
He has sent me to proclaim liberty to captives, sight to the blind,
to let the oppressed go free,
to proclaim a year of favour from the Lord.'

He then rolled up the scroll, gave it back to the assistant and sat down. And all eyes in the synagogue were fixed on him. Then he began to speak to them, 'This text is being fulfilled today even while you are listening'" (Luke 4:17-20, NJB).

The prophets made it unmistakably clear that God's love for Israel was grounded in God's will for a community of justice and righteousness. Righteousness, or uprightness, concerned the character of the people, and justice concerned the structure or order of the nation. Jesus launched his ministry by affirming this, proclaiming good news to the afflicted, liberty to the captives, sight to the blind, freedom to the oppressed, and a year of favor or jubilee when debts were canceled and slaves set free. With this reference to Isaiah, Jesus was saying that the reign of God was at hand, coming alive in works of justice and righteousness in order to bring human life and dignity into its fullness.

God's love, or *agape* love, finally has to do with compassion, stewardship, justice, and solidarity. Peter Henriot, S.J., writes, "When I say I love someone, I want what is best for them. I want their dignity respected, their rights protected, their growth promoted. My love is my commitment to their justice, for that's what dignity, rights, and growth are all about." Henriot says, "If I love someone and want their justice secured, I can't just stop with only a personal response on my part. I must move on to dealing with the structures that oppress or suppress them (economic, political, social, and cultural structures). . . . The definition of action for justice, then, is clear: loving persons so much that I work to change the structures that violate their dignity."[1]

Again we are considering the vision of Christ in others. To see Christ in others and to see their dignity assaulted by injustice is to see God's righteousness mocked. To ignore the root causes for homelessness and hunger, for example, is to mock the reign of God. To be a willing collaborator with racism and sexism is to mock God's will for justice. To live lives of wasteful consumption, doing violence to the earth and its resources, is to ridicule God's will for stewardship. To assent to a national policy of military intervention in Central America is to violate God's greatest commandment to love. Robert McAfee Brown has written that "if we refuse to say No to evil, we cannot say Yes to God."[2]

"All well and good," some would say, "but as it is, my life is as filled and busy as it can possibly get. Rarely do I have time to simply catch up with myself and my family, much less take on any more cares of the world." It cannot be denied that life for many Americans is pressure-packed with the stress of hectic schedules and endless obligations and responsibilities. Where, indeed, is there room for anything or anyone else? Where do we find the energy to change the structures?

There are no easy answers, but there is another way to come to the questions. If we see peacemaking as our response to God's peacegiving and as a central expression of our faith, then it is likely that there can be a reordering of our needs. If we are truly secure in the knowledge of God's forgiveness and we can accept and love our own imperfect selves, then there must be some things we can let go of, masks that can be disposed of, ways in which we can live more simply, freeing up time, money, and emotional energy.

Our checkbooks and calendars reveal the priorities by which we live. How much of the record reflects our call to be compassionate and courageous agents of hope? How much is a record of trivial pursuit? Life, as it is divided up into segments of time—weeks, days, hours, and payroll periods, is not something we own; rather it is a gift from God. Does our use of it reflect an interrelatedness with God's world, with the Christ who is present in the afflicted, captives, and the oppressed?

If our lives are integrated, if the Doing and the Being sides line up, we will do justice and address the structural injustice as we live out our lives in our family, job, and congregation. In other words, it is not simply a matter of taking on more or adding more layers of activity and responsibility. Rather, it is being consistent about who we are, of using time and money to give concrete expression to the values we profess.

I once read of a man who was asked on his eightieth birthday what was the most important lesson he had learned in his long life. His reply was surprisingly simple but profound, dovetailing with what Robert McAfee Brown said about saying No to evil and Yes to God. The octogenarian replied, "I have learned that everytime I say Yes to something, I must say No to something else." To remember this truth can give us direction in the reordering of our lives for peacemaking. To what do we say Yes and to what do we say No?

The Wound of Solidarity

A fundamental questions is: Do we say Yes to the pain of others? Do we let ourselves open to the pain of people who are victims of injustice? Or do we deny the suffering with, "Please don't tell me about the children murdered by the Contras; I cannot take one more thing. Already I have all I can do to keep body and soul together"? John Kavanaugh says of this, "We are deathly afraid of the wound of love. We miss the consolation of our faith because we miss its painful implications."[3] One of these implications certainly must be to say No to some of the distractions of a "thingified" existence, so that our hearts, prayers, and time can be open to the needs of "the least of these" (Matthew 25:31-46). This is love's wound of solidarity.

Solidarity is a word about unity, love, and justice; about being present to the poor and powerless. It is a word that is used in the context of human liberation from systems and policies that deny freedom and dignity. The courageous stand for human rights in communist Poland by Lech Walesa and the independent trade union, Solidarity, come immediately to mind. Dr. Martin Luther King, Jr., Dorothy Day, and the martyred Archbishop Romero of El Salvador are others whose lives were lived in solidarity with the poor and powerless.

Does solidarity have relevance for "regular," bill-paying, church-going, hardworking folks who believe in the tenets of the faith and who are active in their congregations? Unfortunately, solidarity is in the language and thinking of too few of our congregations and parishes. Deeds of mercy we can muster, but deeds of justice and solidarity that change the root reasons for poverty and powerlessness are precious few; too often the power of fear has silenced the power of love. It has no place in church, we say. God must weep over this sad and empty response. Phillip Russell, former Anglican Archbishop of Capetown, South Africa, has said, "You can't pray Our Father without praying for our brothers and sisters, and you can't pray for our brothers and sisters without praying about who they are, where they are, and why they are where they are."[4] The point is well taken—Christian solidarity begins in prayers of confession and intercession.

The word solidarity can have a vagueness, and perhaps to some, even a rhetorical quality if we fail to get specific in its use. Contrary to what some may think, one need not be out on the fringes to live in solidarity with the poor and powerless. Let me cite some examples. I live a rather ordinary middle-class, suburban existence, and yet only the constraints of space limit the listing of people I know who are engaged in solidarity in their (also rather ordinary) lives. The word solidarity makes me think specifically of:

— *Mev*, a creative young teacher who is doing an incredible job teaching her affluent high school students in the suburbs about the roots of economic injustice in Central America. She has even taken groups of them to Haiti and also uses her skills as a photographer to bring the message home.

— *Etta*, a woman with bread-baking skills that the rest of us wish we had, who fused her breadbaking avocation with teaching others about the systemic causes of hunger.

— *Jim*, an educator, whose solidarity takes the form of sacrificial action. In his "accompaniment" with victims of injustice through two-week periods of prayers and fasting, he has been strengthened to change within as well as to work to change the conditions of their injustice.

— *Mary*, who designed a simulation about being on welfare that has been used with members of the Missouri legislature in the advocacy work for welfare reform.

— *Cas*, a builder who teaches the skills of construction and carpentry to people who are hard-core unemployed, working side by side with them.

— *Bolen*, a retired superintendent of schools, who coordinates an Urgent Action Network of people who respond with legislative calls and letters in the areas of the arms race, economic justice, and Central America.

— *Immanuel Lutheran Church*, a congregation of urban poor, with its "Sanctuary, Si!" banner on the front lawn, providing sanctuary to refugees from El Salvador.

These are but a sampling of people from my own experience who have used their skills and passion to do justice and show love, as they "bloom where they're planted." They are, indeed, saying Yes to the pain of others through their acts of solidarity; examples of "regular" folks in whom the power of fear has not silenced the power of love.

However, while there are many other Christian individuals like these, working together in networks and coalitions in acts of solidarity, many must go outside of their own congregations to find the avenues to serve because the corporate will within the congregation to do justice is weak, lacking, or confused. Have our congregations distanced themselves from the anguish of the powerless because they have not themselves heard the Good News? Is our own spiritual poverty locking us out of the House of Love?

Gibson observes that solidarity "emphasizes both the God-given oneness and equal worth of all humanity." He underscores

> the imperative in a sinful, broken world for those committed to realizing shalom to join forces with vigor and determination. . . .[Solidarity] puts caring people, even if they have benefited from unjust structures and attitudes, on the side of those who struggle for liberation, for equal rights, for full inclusion. . . . In our time, it may be a more meaningful term for neighbor love. . . . It lifts up the universality of the love commandment: love every neighbor near and distant. It refuses to let us take the commandment for granted: solidarity costs something. . . . To be in solidarity with the poor and powerless, and with whoever will get involved in God's liberating activity in the present crisis, is for the Christian to stand with Jesus Christ and share his sufferings on behalf of the world that he makes whole.[5]

"He has anointed me to bring the good news to the afflicted . . . liberty to captives, sight to the blind, to let the oppressed go free" (Luke 4:18, NJB). These words give evidence to God's ultimate gift of solidarity with humankind through the life, death, and resurrection of Jesus. They return us finally to our beginning question: Do we say Yes to the pain of others? If we are to be Christian peacemakers breaking the cycles of fear and violence, the call to solidarity is unmistakable.

Equipping Ourselves: Yes to Newness

When people know they have a long journey ahead, they prepare. Planning and equipping can help keep the strangeness of foreign turf from becoming overwhelming; it helps us stay on the course.

Saying Yes to justice and the compassion of solidarity is the beginning of a long journey. Though filled with foreign and sometimes painful and threatening turf, it is a journey of richness and fulfillment with people who are loving and giving. It does require this preparation: coming to a decision to begin. Period. Contrary to a journey of travel in which we equip ourselves before the departure, this is a journey in which equipping ourselves is part of the journey itself.

To equip ourselves we become intentional in learning. We ask questions and search out the answers. Who owns? Who controls? Who pays? Who gets? Who is left out? Who is included? What is the basis for exclusion and inclusion? Who decides what for whom? How do they decide? What are the values? How are they reflected? What religious beliefs support or challenge the situation? And finally: How do we decide who to believe?

The questions and a search for the answers bring us face to face with issues that reflect racism, sexism, elitism, and militarism. Nobody said it would be an easy journey! Learning about these issues is to say Yes to newness and No to some of the usual ways we have thought about things. It is Yes to the willingness to be confused and disturbed in order to come to some new understanding; a willingness to get out of the predictable with our reading, our television viewing, the places we go, and the people with whom we interact. It is an intentional shift from "EZ Listening" to public radio; from *People* and *Self* to the editorial page and the Scriptures; from books on how to increase your power and holdings to books by and about people whose experiences are different from ours. Equipping ourselves is about learning.

"Upsetting!" some would say. Indeed! And that's not necessarily bad. Think, if you will, of a table in the household that, week after week, is used by the family for the papers, magazines, and other assorted information and trivia that never get put away or thrown away. The table seems gradually to take on a life of its own as the stacks and clutter increase, until one day it accidentally gets tipped over, upsetting everything on top. Then a sorting-out must take place. Valued items are rediscovered and appreciated when they emerge from the obsolete and useless things that are finally disposed of; new treasures are found that had been swallowed up by the clutter. Such is some of the upset of saying Yes to the newness of the justice journey. We have to sort through the clutter of assumptions, perceptions, and opinions in the light of new data.

The Lifestyle of More with Less

We said earlier that living in solidarity with the poor and powerless needs to be considered in specific ways. Living out our values in the marketplace and the checkbook opens up unlimited opportunities for specifics. The use of our money is probably the most frequent opportunity that middle-class people have to do justice. What we buy, where we buy, how much we buy, what we do not buy, and where we invest become specific justice decisions. What and who does our money support? How compatible are our consumer habits with the earth's ecological limits? How much of anything do we actually need? Are we indulging in excesses that deny sufficiency for others?

The link between our national delight for fast-food hamburgers and hunger in Brazil exemplifies the lifestyle/justice crunch. In a country of poverty with a crushing national debt, the use of land in Brazil has changed dramatically to provide beef for the U.S. fast-food industry. Tropical rainforests have been cleared for cattle grazing, and land that previously grew table food for Brazilians now fattens cattle for export. As a result, more Brazilians have less food to eat, and the deforestation has resulted in grave soil erosion, claiming badly needed roads to the villages of this impoverished nation. Furthermore, the process of deforestation has even affected the weather patterns, which further impact crop production. "Where's the beef?" indeed!

Our celebrations are yet another aspect for faithfully living out the values of interdependence and solidarity. Milo Thornberry describes celebrations as "ritualized interruptions in daily life, giving it meaning *by reminding us of who we are, where we have been and where we are going*."[6] The excesses of materialism that turn Advent and Christmas into a season that some folks dread is an example of celebrating that contradicts the compassion of solidarity. What changes can we make in the way we celebrate so that our celebrations "remind us of who we are"—brothers and sisters in solidarity with the poor and powerless? It is helpful to know that there are some excellent resources to support people seeking to make these lifestyle changes.[7] What will be discovered in the process of integrating the Being and Doing parts of lifestyle is that, while old habits die hard, the new habits not only benefit others, but ourselves as well. Simplicity, acted on in love and graciousness, evokes joy, wholeness, and even better health!

One more specific item regarding solidarity and the checkbook is our response to organizations doing advocacy and education for systemic change. How might we strengthen their effectiveness? Volunteer work and financial support are welcomed. In my work at the Institute for Peace and Justice, I have seen the dramatic impact that contributors have on the work for peace and justice as well as the enabling effect that the giving relationship has on those who give. Through financial support, people such as the "IPJ Shareholders" are in a partnership, working to address root causes of injustice and defensiveness.

I recall Sister Ann, elderly and diminutive, who has lived a life of sacrificial service. She responded to our institute's need for funds with the desire to ask others. This amazing woman raised over $3,000; in her seventies, she had become a fund raiser! Her solidarity has helped us produce resources for educating others about the causes and ways to address social injustice.

Knowing and Naming the Poor

Solidarity, or compassion, requires both an acknowledgment of our community with all other people and an understanding of what injustice and adversity mean in human terms. We need to be able to have names and faces be part of our understanding. If "them," "the poor," or "people on welfare" are the only names we know, we will miss understanding how, beyond our differences, we are all one body. "In this process of naming and knowing we move past patronizing charity toward the possibility of human community. We find that before *we* named them, they were already named and known by God. . . . We begin to learn humility as we discover the arrogance of our separateness. Who were we to be so far apart in the first place?"[8]

Deeds of mercy provide us with the possibility for establishing a personal connection so that the naming and knowing of community can begin. They are actions that provide material aid and direct services to the victims of injustice and adversity in their needs for the immediate, whether it be food, clothing, utilities, medical supplies, or personal support. Deeds of mercy range all the way from visiting patients at the county hospital and volunteering at the local shelter for homeless people to manning a hot line for threatened farm families, visiting people in prison, and people-to-people programs like sending school supplies to children in Nicaragua.[9]

The blessing that can accompany the ministry of mercy is that those who participate develop a keener understanding, not only of our oneness, but also of realities that have not registered with us before. If we are open, the people have much to teach us, including some things about ourselves, our misconceptions, and our society. We might also discover that one who is economically poor can be spiritually rich. Jesus' ministry was a revelation of God's special love for the poor. Through our relationships with the poor we might experience the Good News in ways we've never known. We can then be strengthened to be more effective agents of hope and change.

"The King will reply, 'I tell you, whenever you did this for one of the least important of these brothers [and sisters] of mine, you did it for me!" (Matthew 25:40). "Without justice, there can be no peace. Without compassion, there can be no justice. Without knowing and naming the poor, there is no true compassion."[10]

Getting to the Causes

Social justice educators often tell the tale of the man who was horseback riding in hill country. As he approached a narrow river that was rushing to lower levels, he came upon a startling scene. There in the river was a baby being carried swiftly downstream. Two people were in the river trying to rescue the child and on the banks of the river were three other babies, surrounded by several other people tending to them. The man could see that these babies had just been rescued too. As the man watched the amazing rescue of the baby that was taking place, another baby came rushing into view. And then another came, and yet another.

The people on the banks were rapidly becoming overwhelmed by the enormity of the task of the increasing rescue operation while tending to the needs of the babies who had already been removed. Clearly, there was not enough help, and the situation was worsening rapidly.

The man hesitated for a moment, trying to decide how he could best help. He was not a good swimmer and he hadn't held a baby in years. Then, just as another baby came within view in the rushing river, the man pulled the reins on his horse. The horse turned and quickly began to gallop along the rocky bank, carrying the man upstream. He called out to the people on the banks, "I'll go upstream to find out what has happened to cause all these babies to come floating down the river."

The tale is simple but effective in explaining the need for deeds of justice. While it was essential for the people on the banks of the river to respond with compassion to the babies in the river, someone was needed to get to the root cause of the problem so that additional babies would be spared being victims. As it was, the needs of the situation were outstripping the resources, and saddest of all, the lives of the babies were in peril.

Like the man riding upstream to find the source of the problem, peacemakers must not only minister to the victims of poverty and injustice; they must also work to change the conditions that produce poverty. Christ not only calls us to feed the hungry; he needs us to go up the river and address the causes of the hunger. We are called both to deeds of mercy and justice.

Mercy says, "I am sorry you are hungry. May I share my food with you?" Solidarity and justice say, "I will walk with you. I will work to help change the cause of your hunger," with the implication, "I am willing to make changes in my own life."

8

Agents of Hope

In the play *Man of LaMancha*, there is a scene in which Cervantes, who has been imprisoned by the Inquisition, is subjected to a cruel mock trial conducted by the other prisoners. They charge him with being "an idealist, a bad poet, and an honest man." One of his accusers, jeering that Cervantes turns his back on life, scoffs: "A man must come to terms with life as it is!"

Answering the charge, Cervantes describes the pain and misery that he has seen in his lifetime: "I have been a soldier and seen my comrades fall in battle. . . . I have held them . . . at the final moment. These were men who saw life as it is, yet they died despairing. No glory, no gallant last words . . . only their eyes filled with confusion, whimpering the question: 'Why?' I do not think they asked why they were dying, but why they had lived."

Cervantes then says something that speaks to the bunker mentality that seems to shape our destiny today: "When life itself seems lunatic, who knows where madness lies? Perhaps to be too practical is madness. To surrender dreams—this may be madness. To seek treasures where there is only trash. Too much sanity may be madness. *And maddest of all, to see life as it is and not as it should be*."[1] [emphasis added]

To be a peacemaker is to see beyond life as it is and to work for life as it should be; valuing truth over data, and justice over the logical acceptance of expediency. To be a peacemaker is to reject the despairing security of a defense budget that pays for Star Wars technology at the sacrifice of health care and housing for the poor and education for our youth. It is to denounce the inhumanity of a national policy that forces people, fleeing from murder and political violence in Central America, to be illegal aliens instead of refugees. It is to deal honestly and creatively with conflicting U.S. and Soviet values and policies in ways that do not require underground nuclear testing or violation of arms control treaties.

Peacemakers must ultimately reject violence as inherent and acceptable for the way people, institutions, and nations live out their lives. Indeed, peacemakers must be agents of hope.

Who Is Violent?

If we are to reject violence we need to be able to discern our own complicity in that which destroys life and human dignity. For this we need clarity on the meaning of violence.

A woman from the Philippines helped me with this. Jean Llorin lives in Quezon City near Manila. She is a Roman Catholic laywoman who helped organize and train people in nonviolence prior to the "Gentle Revolution," which ended the dictatorship of Ferdinand Marcos without gunfire in February, 1986.

Jean shared with me the pain of the Filipino people in the years under the violent Marcos government. She related how the humanity of the people had been repeatedly and brutally denied. Here in the States we have read of the disappearances, murders, and terrible poverty imposed on a people while national resources were being diverted to Marcos and those who supported him. But Jean's definition of violence is one that would give people on all sides cause to pause, for it brings into consideration not only the violence of the perpetrators, but also the response of the victims and those who are present in some way to the violence.

"When you are the barrier between who someone is and who they can become, you are guilty of violence," Jean said. That barrier separating who people are from who they can become can be the violence of systems and apathy as well as psychological abuse or brute force. The way in which people respond to these barriers either perpetuates a cycle of violence or intervenes in that violence, which has already dehumanized both victim and agent of violence. For the victim and those aware of the violence, to be passive or to counter with more violence further denies their own dignity as it contributes to the further dehumanization of the originator of the violence.

The alternative to counterviolence and passivity is active nonviolence. It was used in the Philippine revolution to overthrow Marcos. William Robert Miller describes nonviolence as a way of waging social conflict that is compatible with love, holding the door open to creative and constructive possibilities.[2] Put simply, active nonviolence works for both an end to the evil as well as a recovery of the humanity of both the victims and agents of violence. It is redemptive rather than vengeful, seeking to change that which destroys life and dignity in the hope that unity rather than separation can finally prevail.

By withdrawing support from a government that had become a barrier to their humanity, Jean and thousands of others used the principles of active nonviolence in regaining their dignity. Acknowledging that their passiveness had contributed to the violence of the Marcos government, they exercised their economic power, withdrawing their money from the banks, and boycotting products that supported the Marcos regime. In a stunning witness to nonviolence, thousands of unarmed people overcame the resistance of the heavily armed Philippine army with human barricades on the streets of Manila. In the end, the men in the army were reconciled with the people in a unity of nationhood.

Jean was very clear that because of the value placed on human dignity in the philosophy of nonviolence, it was essential that following his overthrow, Mr. Marcos be treated in a way "that would allow for the possibility for him to recover his humanity." Revenge would have been a barrier to both the agent and the victims. Jean and other leaders of the nonviolent revolution were grateful that he had been allowed a home in Hawaii. Like the impassioned Cervantes, she still had a vision of what life could be for Ferdinand Marcos. She is truly a woman of peace.

To Do Justice

"When you become the barrier between who someone is and who they can become, you are guilty of violence." Never had I heard it put so clearly. Despair and apathy to injustice are that kind of violence, for they give tacit consent to existing barriers that prevent people from being fully human. Conversely, to respond to injustice with loving creativity that seeks to remove the barriers is to affirm the unity of humankind.

Through deeds of justice we work to change the systems, structures, policies, and practices that do violence to people, either by willful destruction of life or by institutional forces that diminish human dignity. This institutional violence can be as deadly as overt violence. A high infant mortality rate in a community, for example, is a telling indicator of inadequate health care, unemployment, and often racism. In South Africa's rural areas, the infant mortality rate is over two hundred deaths per thousand of black infant births. It is only thirteen per thousand of white infants.[3] The peacemaker has a different vision of what life should be for those black children of South Africa or for the black infants of St. Louis, who also suffer a high mortality rate. To have the vision is to also be committed to changing the conditions, removing the barriers of injustice that breed fearfulness, defensiveness, and violence.

This is to go upstream, sometimes alone. And it is here, precisely at the point where more voices of solidarity are needed that the ranks of peacemakers thin out. It is here that the fear of pain and powerlessness begins to intrude; where people discover what kind of security they do, in fact, claim.

"What difference could I possibly make?" is an often-asked question, reflecting the powerlessness that some see as inherent to situations of injustice. One answer comes by way of a tale about a man who was seen on a beach filled with thousands of fish that had been carried by the tide onto the beach to a certain death. The man was picking up fish, one by one, casting them back into the sea. A passerby mocked his modest efforts, in view of the enormity of the problem. Tossing back another fish, the man replied, "I can't throw them all back, but I know *this* one will feel better!"

There is also another answer, a more basic one, to "What difference could I possibly make?" It is that Christ calls us to faithfulness. We who are loved and forgiven have been charged to witness to faith and hope by doing these things that bring wholeness, unity, and reconciliation to the world. We have been called to help end the violence. James says it this way, "Show me how anyone can have faith without actions. I will show you my faith by my actions" (James 2:18). The youth choir in my church sings it in another way: "You can't be a beacon if your light don't shine!" If our beacon is hope, our light will be the deeds of justice.

How do we let our light shine? How will we clarify our relationship to God and to Caesar? What do we do after we have prayed, studied, and reflected? Like Cervantes, hopeful folks have a vision of life as it should be. Their hope is the active arm of love, changing the evidence that gives cynics a profession. How will we get specific about changing the evidence? What deeds of justice will we do?

Deeds of justice should be considered, not out of guilt but because they are freeing. As we seek to free victims from the oppressive systems of fear, we ourselves are freed from the fear of intimidation and our own powerlessness. Deeds of justice free us from false securities as we discover the power within us and the true security of love and truth.

Because the unending lists of injustices will forever outstrip our personal resources of time and energy to respond, it is important for the peacemaker to consider some things:

Be aware of your motivation. Guilt or trying to please others may suffice for awhile, but they won't sustain us for the long haul. Both motives are based in a fear of the Imperfect Self rather than the love of people, truth, and justice; they are a contradiction to peacemaking.

Select deeds that feel right. No person is called to do everything. We are called to faithfulness and that includes making sure that our deeds are integrated with our feelings. Wholeness is a value of peacemaking.

If action makes you feel afraid, examine the source of your fear. Can you discern what area of security is being threatened? Is this a legitimate fear? Can it be put to rest?

Wherever possible, act in community. Find others who share your concerns and who can be mutually supportive.

Keep balance in your life—balance between acting and reflecting, speaking and silence, doing and being, working and playing, seriousness and laughter. Recall that even Jesus withdrew from the people who needed him in order to pray (Matthew 14:22-23).

Try new ventures; step out on your faith. You will not be alone; God strengthens those who ask.

What does it finally come down to? What are some of the ways we can share in the work for justice and peace? How can we be agents of hope? There are many possibilities open to us; what follows are some of them.

Speaking Out—Share convictions with family and friends, sometimes a hard thing to do. Write letters to the editor; signing your name is owning your values. Wear symbols of your beliefs, such as a button or ribbon; symbols elicit conversation. In other words, come out of hiding; private opinions are just that—private. Change in public policy does not evolve in a vacuum of expression.

Voting for Justice and Peace—Examine the track record of the candidates for public service. Look at their stands on the issues of justice. Consider candidates whose records reflect the Doing aspects of interdependence. (See page 45.) They will need your vote, money, and time. Values require substance.

Educating Others; Being a Conduit of Information—Initiate a study group or a dialogue. Participate in people-to-people programs. Share books, leaflets, and action opportunities; tell others, including the uninitiated, about forums and speakers in your community. Break new ground! You won't be the first "voice crying in the wilderness"; it is a timeless calling.

Lobbying and Doing Advocacy—Write or contact your congressperson frequently on specific issues of injustice or legislation relating to it. This involves keeping a close eye on the times, watching to see how national policy affects the poor and powerless, whether it be in your own community, your state, the nation, or other countries. Support the advocacy efforts of others with the letters, calls, and money they need for effectiveness. Amos and Jeremiah are among the cloud of witnesses who will be cheering for you.

Community Organizing—Work with others in the community who are organized around local justice issues such as housing, health care, utility rates, or voter registration. Attend hearings, help circulate petitions, get to know those who represent you in the state capitol.

Networking—Connect with other groups and organizations sharing your values and concerns; participate in urgent action networks. The issues are many; networks and coalitions make it possible to communicate and respond with timeliness to the wide range of peace and justice issues. Many times local justice issues are connected to national and global problems; "think globally, act locally." If you are at a loss for a place to begin, present yourself as a volunteer to the local women's self-help center, a shelter for the homeless, or a peace and justice center.

To stay in touch with current developments and legislative needs in areas such a nuclear weapons, apartheid, economic justice, or Central America, call the national hotlines for recorded messages.[4] Here you will learn things that are often not in the media, as well as action opportunities that are needed.

Protesting Publicly—Object publicly to policies of injustice by participating in petition drives, letter writing campaigns, vigils, marches, and demonstrations. Remember that this is a fruit of democracy and, when done nonviolently, it is an act of responsible citizenship. To be credible, the protest should offer alternative avenues to the situation at hand.

In acts of public protest, seek to integrate the Being and Doing aspects of love discussed earlier. Vulnerability, truthfulness, mutuality, compassion, courage, and righteous anger make up the mosaic. Vengefulness is a contradiction.

Praying—Accompany the poor and oppressed in your prayer life, and seek divine guidance in your own struggles of courage and conscience.

Resisting Structures of Violence—Withdraw cooperation and support from the forces of fear and violence that destroy life and dignity, and that deny God's purpose in both the lives of the victims and the perpetrators. War-tax resistance and sanctuary are two examples; there are many others that are less visible, but very important.

Models of Nonviolent Resistance

If, as we noted earlier, miracles are what happen when God's justice and righteousness are present, we can see evidence of the miracles birthed by active nonviolence. Martin Luther King, Jr. brought about the miracle of social change through nonviolent action in the 60s. There have also been other times and places when nonviolent resistance has brought forth God's miracles of *shalom*. There was the Underground Railroad that transported slaves to freedom; Gandhi's salt march to the sea; Rosa Parks' refusal to sit in the back of the bus; and a seven-year abstinence from Nestlé chocolate bars. The miracles that came forth: slavery became obsolete in the United States, India attained nationhood, the Civil Rights movement was born, and a multinational corporation stopped using deadly marketing practices on Asian and African mothers.

Today there are new peacemakers who are withdrawing cooperation and support from systems that destroy life and dignity. Through their nonviolent action they are working to end cycles of fear that deny the humanity of both the victims and the agents of violence. We find these miracles in divestiture from the interests that support South African apartheid, in the Sanctuary movement, in withdrawal from nuclear related jobs, in conscientious objection to Selective Service registration, in war-tax resistance, and in civil disobedience at defense facilities.

Withdrawal of cooperation and support from that which denies life and dignity also takes place daily in the lives of ordinary people who recognize that God's vision of wholeness and dignity requires consistency. In addition to acts that risk arrest or threaten income, there are other acts in which the level for personal risk isn't high, but that still require people to go against what is expected or demanded by the culture.

Active nonviolence takes place when someone who tells a racist joke is met with total silence; when a man withdraws his membership from a private business club that still discriminates. Nonviolence takes place at the supermarket when grapes aren't purchased because people support the farmworkers in their battle against pesticides. It is the refusal to buy war toys for our children. It takes place when a viewer writes the program director of the local television station saying, "Last night I changed the channel because your program during family viewing time glorified war and violence as a way to solve differences. I reject that value system."

Nonviolent action seeks to change that which destroys life and human dignity. It is the beacon's shining light. However, as Miller notes, nonviolence "has no intrinsic power to heal and to build anew. For this we must look beyond nonviolence to active, agapic love and reconciliation."[5]

Love One Another

"*You did not choose me; I chose you and appointed you to go and bear much fruit, the kind of fruit that endures. And so the Father will give you whatever you ask of him in my name. This, then, is what I command you: love one another*" (John 15:16,17).

Christ has called us to intervene in the cycles of defensiveness and violence; we've been charged with changing the conditions that breed insecurity and fear. The Gospel of John, especially chapters 13—17, is a source of strength to those who answer this call. In those chapters Jesus clearly teaches that to be claimed by God is to be claimed to love. Jesus knew better than we how revolutionary this ministry of love could be. He knew that the love that relieves suffering and poverty by changing the conditions of fear was on a collision course with the world's vested interests. He knew that there would be times when we would feel intimidated, discouraged, and alone, ready to despair; that sometimes we would fail or be inhibited by our fear. For all this he promised the presence of God's Helper in the certain struggle. "The Helper will come—the Spirit, who reveals the truth about God and who comes from the Father" (John 15:26).

What peacemaking finally comes down to is a question of faith. Do we believe in Christ's promises? Do we believe that we are forgiven, that we belong to God? Can we receive Christ's peace? "Peace I bequeath to you, my own peace I give you, a peace which the world cannot give, this is my gift to you. Do not let your hearts be troubled or afraid" (John 14:27, NJB). Do we trust in the enabling power of the Holy Spirit?

Jürgen Moltmann dispels any naiveté that might creep into our thinking about what God's peace will mean in our lives. Moltmann writes, "Peace with God means conflict with the world, for the goad of the promised future stabs inexorably into the flesh of every unfulfilled present."[6] To say Yes to God's peace is to be forever impassioned with a vision of what life can be for all people; it is to say Yes to the pain of suffering love. Finally, to say Yes to Christ's claim of love is to say Yes to justice and righteousness and to say No to the world's fear and violence.

How shall we reply?

9

Risking Something Active and Genuine

"*Our love must be not just words or mere talk but something active and genuine*" (1 John 3:18, NJB).

John counsels us that love needs to be expressed in more than just words and mere talk; rather, that it be "something active and genuine." Peacemaking, if it is to be faithful to Christ's call to love, is not a word, a project, or even a strategy. It is finally a way of life, removing barriers that separate who we are from whom we can become, so that we can become reconciled with God, ourselves, those around us, the earth, and humankind.

How does this vision come alive in "something active and genuine"? What will be the characteristics of faithful peacemaking?

— *In spirituality*—repentant, disarmed of fear, trusting in God's grace and promises;

— *In relationships*—caring, truthful, nurturing community and sharing power;

— *In lifestyle*—sharing and conserving; protecting the earth;

— *In conflict*—respecting the dignity of the adversary; negotiating the issues, seeking areas of common security, rejecting violence and revenge;

— *In citizenship*—participating; challenging and risking when the government violates its moral integrity;

— *In solidarity with the poor and powerless*—compassionate, risking security to change root causes of pain and injustice.

My former pastor had the privilege of hearing Archbishop Tutu preach in Chicago in 1986. He related that Tutu said to the gathered clergy, "I believe that today God is asking us, 'Can you help me?' " God has asked that question of believers across the centuries. The apostle Paul, like Tutu, answered that call, working at great risk to witness to the Good News. So secure was his faith that he was able to write to the Christians in Rome that he was certain that "there is nothing in all creation that will ever be able to separate us from the love of God which is ours through Christ Jesus our Lord" (Romans 8:39).

Paul's assurance of the security of God's love is a source of strength when we begin to come to terms with the question, "Can you help me?" It is the security of God's love that will enable us to move from fear and defensiveness to hope and vulnerability. For it is then that our perspective is changed and the questions are reframed. Instead of wondering "What difference can I make?" and "How will I protect myself?" we begin to consider "How am I to be faithful to God's will for justice? What can I do to nurture compassion and reconciliation? What can I risk to counteract violence?"

By considering what we can risk, we also consider the sources of our fear. Each time we are able to risk something, we strengthen our faith and trust in God's abiding love. When we find there are things that we cannot risk, despite sincere intentions, it is helpful to honestly ask what it is that we fear; what areas of our security are threatened by taking the risk? This is an ongoing struggle. It is important that we continue to ask ourselves the questions and be assured that God is with us in these private times of conscience.

The questions that become the hardest to answer are those that reveal areas where our inability to risk contributes to the basic insecurity of others, when through our own fearfulness and needs for ersatz security we participate in denying basic needs of other people. Taxes, jobs, comfort, and convenience—these are realities that trigger hard questions. "There is nothing in all creation that will ever be able to separate us from the love of God" (Romans 8:39). God will sustain us in our search for the truth.

Risking is part of the journey of peacemaking. Depending on where we are on the journey, the risks vary. The following presents a spectrum of some of the risks of as well as some areas of our security or insecurity. Which risks can we consider at this point in the journey? What areas of security are tied to those risks that seem to be beyond us now? Where are our pockets of fear? Where are our strengths?

Some Risks of Peacemaking	*Areas of Security or Insecurity*
Interior: letting in the	
pain and confusion	
Family: upset of the equilibrium;	Spiritual and interior
trying new ways	life
Friends and colleagues: dis-	
approval, being misunderstood	
Lifestyle challenges:	
openness to new experiences	Relationships
sharing power	
scaling down comfort, leisure	
and possessions (need vs.	
desire)	Lifestyle
sharing and conserving	
increased giving	
reordering time priorities	
Vulnerability in public	Employment
statements and actions	
Economic implications:	
different job	
reduced income	Personal Freedom
"assured future" not viable	
Legal implications of nonviolent	
resistance:	
IRS audits; fines	Basic needs
government harassment	
arrest; trial	
imprisonment	
loss of job	Safety
Personal safety in jeopardy	

To struggle with the questions is to seek after faithfulness. It is to remember we are always "in process," or as a friend of mine says, "God's not through with us yet." Guilt has no home here; repentance, faith, and newness are the way of love.

At the very beginning we noted Jim Wallis' statement that fear is the greatest enemy of the faith and its final contradiction. We have sought to discover how that plays out in the spiritual life, the life of relationships, and the social order. We have seen how the knowledge or experience of being loved and valued intervenes in the cycles of defensiveness and violence that are spawned by fear. And we have concluded that peacemaking is a witness of hope that changes the conditions that cause people to feel fearful and threatened. It is an empowerment of love.

If we are to confirm God's will for love and justice by the lives we live, we must finally wrestle with the questions of risk and faith. What can our love risk for justice and peace? Can we risk being honest with ourselves? Can we risk accepting God's love and grace and letting it transform us? Can we risk forgiving and accepting ourselves? Can we risk disagreement, internal upset, and disapproval? Can we risk changing our use of time? Can we risk praying for our enemies, including the everyday variety? Can we risk forgiveness? Can we risk being claimed by God rather than Caesar? Finally, can we risk witnessing to the Good News by living lives of hope and nonviolence?

"*Blessed are the peacemakers: they shall be recognised as children of God*" (Matthew 5:9, NJB).

Part III

The Peacemaking Congregation

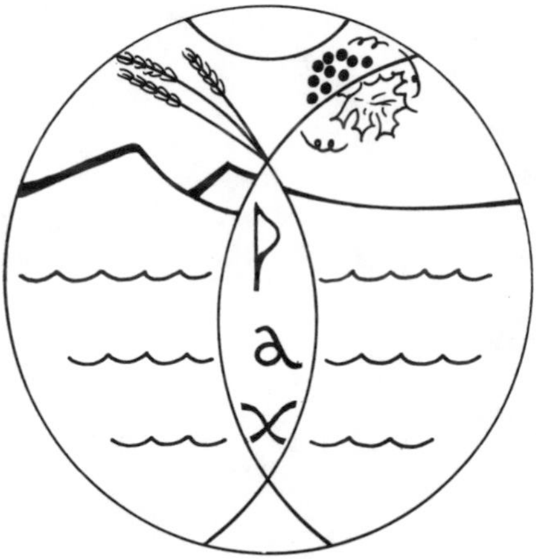

10

Attitudes for a Congregation's Peacemaking and Justice Seeking

A change in the nature of nuclear weapons in the early 1980s altered the context in mainline congregations for addressing social issues. Multiple warheads, the MX missile, and the Trident submarine were some of the evidences that the nuclear arms race had veered into a spiral of increasing vulnerability for people everywhere. Two responses to this new state of urgency directly touched the lives of people in the pews. One was a pastoral letter on war and peace, *The Challenge of Peace*, by the National Conference of Catholic Bishops. The other was a film, *The Last Epidemic*, which gave a wide audience to the national effort of Physicians for Social Responsibility to educate people about the dangers of nuclear war. Until then, social action had receded to almost imperceptible levels in many congregations that had been touched by the controversies surrounding the Civil Rights movement of the 60s and the Vietnam War in the 70s.

But the concerns raised by the bishops' letter and *The Last Epidemic* strengthened the drive for a freeze on nuclear weapons, involving many people from mainline denominations. Issues of social action, as it had been called in earlier years, now had personal relevance for middle-class people because the new weaponry posed questions having to do with both jobs and survival. Social action, which had gone below the surface as a priority, came forth again, recast in a consciousness that was asking fundamental questions about faith, nuclear weapons, and social justice. "What constitutes a secure nation?" became a harder question to answer for people of faith as the new weapons forced budget choices that curtailed public health care, food programs, and housing for the poor. Many, too, were at moral odds with the nation's first-strike or counterforce defense policy, which was in itself a contradiction of terms.

As a result, today one will find an encouraging array of excellent resources at conferences, meetings, and denominational gatherings for congregations to use in their study of the issues of peace and justice. The arms race, Central America, apartheid, parenting for peace and justice, and conflict resolution are but a few of the topics addressed by these program aids. Furthermore, leadership in many of the denominations is speaking and acting with courage on economic justice, sanctuary, and nonviolent resistance. Judicatories and dioceses, too, are taking positions that call national policy into question.

Yet in spite of all the commissions, task forces, resource and staff development about the peace issues, most local parishes and congregations still do not reflect a peace priority in their worship, program, or outreach. Robert Gribbon of the Alban Institute has collected data since 1983 that corroborates this. Commenting on the documents and pastoral letters of major denominations, he observes, "We see little of this being translated into sustained visible activity in local congregations."[1]

There is ample evidence of a fear of the peace priority and a distancing from it by many local congregations. Both clergy and laity share in the stance of timidity. "Peacemaking, to me, is war!" is the way one man from a suburban congregation in LaGrange, Illinois, put it. His perception confirmed what I found in an ecumenical survey on the status of peacemaking in forty congregations, where the fear of conflict and polarization over peace and justice was a recurring theme. Furthermore, fear for jobs, fear of the Russians, fear of not being patriotic, of rejection, of diminishing financial support, and of inadequacy figure into situations where church people are denying themselves the blessing of a climate of faith to explore the questions and conflicts that are raging within their hearts about nuclear war and the difficult issues of justice.

This is in itself a contradiction of the fundamental need for wholeness and integration in our lives and of the way that a congregation can make this real. In the context of true Christian community, the congregation creates an environment of faith where we can share, be confused, disagree, weep, struggle, and find hope together. In that context, we are more than engineers, teachers, business owners, machinists, nurses, and attorneys. We are also sisters and brothers united by the love of the God of grace, called to bring the fruits of that love to others. Gribbon says it well: "If we take individuals seriously, we will create contexts into which people can bring all their hopes, fears, stories, commitments, and ideas. When we allow all of reality to be dealt with in the religious context we find that both issues and people are transformed."[2]

However, it is within a climate that denies this full expression of Christian community that peacemakers often find themselves in their congregations. For them, both clergy and laity, the efforts to make peacemaking an integral part of the life of the congregation is a lonely endeavor of frustration and of being misunderstood. Many who have tried in vain to work through these dilemmas of faith have abandoned any expectation of response by their congregation or parish, choosing instead to act through ecumenical and secular efforts. Their dedication and talents are an enormous loss to the local churches. One woman, a devout Roman Catholic who invests a lot of time ecumenically in peace work, told me that she and her husband had met with so much rebuff in the parish, that they had decided "to stop spinning our wheels at the parish level and to spend time where it would be more productive." Though they still attend their parish, their gifts and commitment to peace and justice are finding expression elsewhere.

Experience with local congregations suggests that many times peacemaking is not an intentional part of the church's life not only because of fear but simply because there is no vision of what peacemaking is or how it is given expression by the local church. One pastor's response reflects, I believe, the inadequacy and powerlessness that many well-intentioned people feel. He commented on the vitality and faithfulness of people in his parish but noted that there was no conscious work related to peacemaking. He observed that "the issues of peacemaking and the action to respond to them are impossible to effectively accomplish because they are so immense and seemingly impossible to handle." His comment reflects the sentiments of many.

It is in knowledge of these realities that we approach the subject of the peacemaker in the parish or congregation. As peacemakers we need to stay in touch with the assurance that we are loved, forgiven, and accepted by a gracious God, whose will for justice and peace was given expression in the life of Jesus. This connectedness with our source of security will affect the attitudes and feelings we bring to our peacemaking—attitudes that are consistent with the knowledge of being loved, and attitudes that will help us to be more effective in that which we are called to do and to be.

Respecting Differences

"We must love them both; those whose opinions we share and those whose opinions we reject. For both have laboured in search of the truth, and both have helped us in finding it." (St. Thomas Aquinas)[3]

We must begin with an acknowledgment and respect for differences and know that differences preclude any presumption on our part of "how things will come out." If you were to ask all the people in your church who profess to care about peace to place themselves at some point on an imaginary line that had Daniel Berrigan at one end and Phyllis Schlafly at the other end, it would be folly to think everyone would rush to the same point on the line. We are people of different experiences, different heritages, and different mixes of fear—all of which have a bearing on our place on the line.

Part of the essence of peacemaking is to respect people, regardless of where they stand on that line. A test of our respect is our ability to avoid labeling or pigeonholing them; nobody fits totally into one neat package. To label or dismiss people as "conservative," "liberal," or with some other cultural shorthand is to limit our perception of their humanity, and therefore, to limit the possibilities for finding common ground. Faithfulness requires that we reject this type of thinking and remember that which unites us even in our diversity within the body of Christ. There are people with whom we will never agree and with whom we have serious theological and ethical differences. But, as much as we are able to muster, we need to separate the people from the issues and remember to see the image of Christ in them. Openness and vulnerability begin here!

There will be times when, despite our commitment to this very concrete opportunity for living the nonviolent life, we will be disappointed and very possibly hurt by hostility. We must be willing to try to handle hostility and frustration in creative ways. To respond in ways that keep open the possibility for growth and reconciliation is to be faithful. Christ didn't say "Blessed are the *peacelovers*"; he said "*peacemakers*." He gave the tipoff nearly two thousand years ago that there was real work to be done.

Sharing the Common Ground

While affirming the theology that says Christians are "in the world but not of the world," I have always felt uncomfortable with church talk on Sunday that speaks of "going out into the world" on Monday. Somehow it suggests a spirit of separation. The fact of the matter is that we who make up the body of Christ are integral parts of that world we speak of "going out into." Furthermore, we bring with us *into* our church life the baggage of our experiences in that world.

We who come together as the church are elderly people who lived through the great Depression; we are veterans who remember the power of the Third Reich and a war that was ended by an atomic bomb. We are families who established homes and habits in the 1960s when newness and abundance were taken as the norm. We who worship on Sunday mornings are a people who were hurt and divided by the Vietnam War. We are people of color who see the inconsistencies of national promise and fulfillment. We are the unemployed and underemployed, living on the edge of uncertainty; we are women who disagree with each other about liberation. We are business people who must meet a bottom line; young professionals who understand power but who feel powerless in avoiding a nuclear war. Some of us are pacifists; many are people whose job security depends on military contracts. We are youth anxiously searching for signs of promise and purpose, and children who still sing "Jesus Loves Me," often living with only one parent.

Indeed we are a diverse people who bring all that we are to the act of worship and the life of the congregation. It is within this diversity of experiences, needs, and expectations that we are a people called to peacemaking; called to make God's will for *shalom* real in ourselves and in others. We are blessed with a oneness in Christ who has loved and redeemed us, and who has asked us to bring the Good News of God's will for justice, love, and reconciliation to all people. It is upon this common ground of faith that we, with our differences, take up the task of peacemaking. If we can begin our peacemaking with the faith we share, rather than with the differences that have been shaped by our varied experiences, we can take up the task together.

Through prayer, study, and interaction with people of varied experiences and points of view, we will be able to let in the pain of others and discern the implications of our faith in the present day. We may not be able to find one single way to respond as a congregation to a given issue, but we will be able to find things we can do in common that will lead to other opportunities for growth, community, peacemaking, and justice seeking. As we seek common ground where people can act together on their commitment for peace and justice, we will honor each other's integrity and appreciate differences.

This means that we cannot enter into congregational peacemaking with some preconceived notion of outcomes or with an agenda to impose on the "unenlightened"; we are enablers to discovery. Almost immediately we will be tested by our needs for control. I recall a pastor at an ecumenical peace seminar several years ago who was deeply disturbed that his church council would not sanction his use of the pulpit to speak to the congregation about endorsing the Nuclear Weapons Freeze. He seemed angry and a little bitter about it. The congregation, which was a city church of both blacks and whites, had a long and consistent record of being generously involved in many aspects of justice within the community, involving itself in ways that many affluent churches have never considered. The pastor, who was new to the congregation, had made the mistake of presuming how this particular issue should turn out, and in effect denied the other significant work of peacemaking in which the congregation was already engaged.

At that same seminar a man from Washington, D.C. described an incredible process of peacemaking in his Methodist congregation where Pentagon staffers, corporate people, and some committed pacifists had forged a working peace task force. Rather than beginning with their differences, which obviously were many, they began from the common ground they shared in terms of their faith and its implications for their lives. They discovered a specific justice project on hunger that they could all address and in the course of bringing that project to fruition within the congregation, they enlarged their common ground and grew in their understanding of the implications of their faith. In the evolving process, this peace task force of diverse people continued to find new ways to work together in their call to peacemaking and justice seeking.

Meeting People Where They Are

To say that we cannot enter into peacemaking by imposing our own agenda is also to say that we meet people where they are. What are the fears, concerns, and felt needs of the people in the parish? It has been said that you can't change what you don't love. It has also been said that you can't love what you don't know. It would seem that there is wisdom in linking those ideas. Furthermore, change, love, and knowing imply listening and feeling. Alfred Krass counsels, "To have good news for people means we've heard their bad news. Only when we know their concerns can we discern God's word as it might come to them in their situation. To speak requires prior hearing."[4]

Listening to their fears and learning what is troubling people does not mean that we can never get beyond those fears. It does mean that if their fears are not heard or considered, we will rarely get beyond them. Listening to fears will give insight into how to make peacemaking relevant to the life of the people, for by definition, peacemaking seeks to address those things that breed insecurity and fear. Fears can provide the bridges for relating to the peace and justice issues.

For example, in a community where defense contracts not only put bread and butter on the table but in effect make it possible for a church to pay its pastor and retire its mortgage through the stewardship of people employed in the defense industry, job security is a real and legitimate concern affecting everyone. Nothing is to be served by ignoring that reality or by failing to acknowledge the impact it has, not only on the defense industry employees, but on the entire congregation and community. This needs to be considered in determining how the congregation will explore the faith questions presented by the arms race.

Understanding defensiveness can also help us to meet people where they are. When we encounter defensiveness in the congregation we need to *stop and think* rather than let it trigger counter-defensiveness within ourselves. Defensiveness has a message for us: It says that something is being threatened, some area of security is in jeopardy. When we sense messages of defensiveness in others we might draw upon the determiners of fear and insecurity that are found in the spiritual life, the life of relationships, and the social order to try to understand the situation. (See chart after page 32.) What is the area of security that seems to be threatened? How is this being expressed in feelings, attitudes, behavior? How are others being affected?

Some further questions are also suggested:

— Is this person's defensiveness evoking defensiveness in me? If so, why do I feel threatened?

— Is there anything in this person's behavior that reminds me of my own dark side; something that I fear or don't like in myself? Can understanding this about myself help me to get beyond my own counter-defensiveness?

— Is there some way that I can help to reduce the level of fear or contribute to a climate of security? How can I reassure, affirm, or otherwise be present to the situation?

— Is there something specific I can do to prevent polarization?

When we learn to listen to the fears, we will gain in our understanding of where to begin, for peacemaking considers the causes of fear and defensiveness.

Patience

In an age when "instant," "immediate," and "now" are marketable values, the attitude of patience becomes almost obsolete. Computers, microwaves, satellites, and 727 jets make the present moment in our lives capable of going infinitely beyond our own little time and space. The high-tech culture gives daily reinforcement to an expectation for immediate access to information, unlimited problem-solving, and instant results. In such a context, where reality is defined by data base systems and cost effectiveness, long-haul patience becomes expendable and relegated to the back of consciousness. In such a climate we stand to lose clear perception of this quality that is needed for wholeness.

Some may even question if patience is an attitude that has any place in the work for justice and peace. The nuclear emergency is obvious, and who would have the effrontery to tell homeless persons in winter that they must be more patient? Indeed, is there a place for patience as an attitude in peacemaking?

"Bearing pains or trials calmly or without complaint" is not the only definition for the word "patient"; this is not the attitude of which we speak. The definition that applies to our peacemaking is "*steadfast despite opposition, difficulty, or adversity*."[5] Steadfast are the peacemakers; faithful and persevering. Being patient is part of the job description.

This attitude of steadfast faithfulness is not without biblical precedent, something we need to recall when the program on Nicaragua that we had worked so hard to present yields a turnout of only five people. Consider the opposition Amos must have encountered when he said, "You people hate anyone who challenges injustice and speaks the whole truth in court. You have oppressed the poor and robbed them of their grain. . . . You persecute good men, take bribes, and prevent the poor from getting justice in the courts" (Amos 5:10-12). Imagine what it took for him to get up and go to work each day!

Consider Jeremiah's adversity, "I wish I had a place to stay in the desert where I could get away from my people. They are all unfaithful, a mob of traitors. They are always ready to tell lies; dishonesty instead of truth rules the land" (Jeremiah 9:2-3). And we think we are uniquely discouraged!

The prophets and the disciples lived lives of long-haul patience to teach about God's will for love and justice for all. And the fact that today we are a church bears testimony to the steadfastness of the early Christians.

Alfred Krass, a United Church of Christ pastor, warns us that meaningful change in people's attitudes takes a long time:

> Preachers and teachers are subject to an occupational hazard: overestimation of the impact of their teaching. . . .

> Learning proceeds in little steps, over a long period of time. People must test their learning little by little. Over months and years they acquire confidence and trust. Positive reinforcements give them the courage to go a step farther. . . . To midwife such change takes patience, love for your people, and hope. Even with that, it'll only happen in fits and starts.[6]

While we must not lose our holy rage over the violence and suffering inflicted by unjust systems, we need to bring patience to the work of reaching the hearts and minds of those in our congregation who could share in transforming those systems. The fact that in earlier times our own fear prevented us from being open to truths in which we now find ourselves engaged is something to remember. And before we get too discouraged with the slow pace of others, we need to acknowledge how cautious we ourselves are in being touched by the prophets of today. We who would change others are, for the most part, distanced from the poor, the wounded, and the suffering, who have much to teach us about the nature of God. This brings us back to the One who risked ultimate patience: "God loved the world so much that he gave his only Son, so that everyone who believes in him may not die but have eternal life" (John 3:16). God, we believe. Help our unbelief, and bless us with your patience.

Confidence in the Promises

"*Remain united to me, and I will remain united to you. A branch cannot bear fruit by itself; it can do so only if it remains in the vine. In the same way you cannot bear fruit unless you remain in me. I am the vine and you are the branches. Whoever remains in me, and I in him, will bear much fruit; for you can do nothing without me*" (John 15:4-5).

It is nearly impossible for those of us who have so much "stuff" to acknowledge dependency; it goes against every ethic we've learned. And yet, here is Jesus telling his disciples that as the branches are to the vine, so are we to his sustenance. "For you can do nothing without me." It is not a threat; it simply states the reality that we are incomplete and unfruitful selves apart from the vine, but that as branches united with the vine we will bear much fruit. Jesus makes clear that love is the mark of fruitfulness: "I chose you and appointed you to go and bear much fruit, the kind of fruit that endures. And so the Father will give you whatever you ask of him in my name. This, then, is what I command you: love one another" (John 15:16-17). Chapters 14, 15, and 16 of John are rich with Jesus' assurances that we will not be alone in acting on the great commandment to love others. We can take confidence in Christ's promise of the Helper's presence in our peacemaking.

The Statement of Faith of the United Church of Christ affirms that God promises to all who trust, "forgiveness of sins and fullness of grace, courage in the struggle for justice and peace." We who are loved and forgiven can take confidence, regardless of denomination, in those promises; so much confidence, in fact, that we can find ways to become peacemaking congregations. *Confidence in the promises of faith will allow us to stop presuming that we cannot struggle together to discover the implications for faithfulness in our lives and the lives of our congregations. As members of a community of love, we will care about each other so much that we will acknowledge and address the problems that have been barriers to a deeper fellowship.*

Our confidence need not be grounded in unrealistic expectation of total knowledge, perfectly developed skills or abilities, and no conflict. If we waited for those attributes we would never get on with our peacemaking. Our confidence will be rooted in the common ground of Father God's redeeming love for his children—children who live in a world where there is only one physician for every 1,030 people, while there is one soldier for every forty-three people. We will act in the confidence of Mother God's love for her children living in a world where one in four goes hungry and where one adult in three cannot read and write, as the nations spend $800 billion a year for military programs.[7] (*That is $800,000,000,000!*) We will be confident in the knowledge that the man Jesus who cared about little children in Judea wants us to do all we are able, so that the humanity of poor children living in our hometowns is affirmed in good health care, nourishing food, and a warm place to live.

We will take confidence that in God's will for justice and righteousness there is a place for us to bring hope by easing the reasons for fear. Robert McAfee Brown puts it directly and honestly, reflecting on Isaiah 61:1-4, "God wants justice? Then act justly. God wills the building up of ancient ruins? Then break out the block and tackle, the cement mixers, the trowels, and get to work. God wants comfort for those who mourn? Then dispense comfort yourself, share a new vision and a new hope."[8] May we serve together in the confidence of God's promises.

11

Leadership with a Vision

From Paul's letters to the churches:

"*Do not conform yourselves to the standards of this world, but let God transform you inwardly by a complete change of your mind*" (Romans 12:2).

"*Do your best to preserve the unity which the Spirit gives by means of the peace that binds you together. There is one body and one Spirit, just as there is one hope to which God has called you*" (Ephesians 4:3-4).

"*We have many parts in the one body, and all these parts have different functions. In the same way, though we are many, we are one body in union with Christ, and we are all joined to each other as different parts of one body. So we are to use our different gifts in accordance with the grace that God has given us*" (Romans 12:4-6).

At the concluding session of a summer institute in which I participated last year, one of the worship leaders offered these questions for reflection: Where were we; where are we now? Who were we; who are we now? Where are we going; what will our future be?

As we begin to determine the nature of peacemaking in our local churches, we can answer: We were estranged and separated; we are now forgiven and reconciled. We were fearful, unaccepting of ourselves, and defensive; we are now disarmed of heart and vulnerable, seeking ways to be faithful and just. As agents of hope, we will help create a future that honors God's will for *shalom*.

— We know that God is the author of peace, creating peace through righteousness. Justice is the condition of this peace, giving it life and structure.

— We know that Jesus, in his ministry, death, and resurrection, is the Revelation of God's peace. Validated in the resurrection, his teaching and suffering on behalf of the poor and outcast have become the universal ministry for all who would follow him.[1]

— We know that the Holy Spirit is God's enabler for peace, sent to help us to honor God's creation of peace by doing the work of love and justice.

— Finally, we know that as the church we are God's people in a covenant of peace, called to be a community of justice: "servant of the Servant Lord," agent of the Good News, and partner of the disregarded.[2]

And now our task is to imagine what miracles of God's justice and righteousness can be born in our local congregations. What is the vision for peacemaking and justice seeking at the Church of New Beginnings? How do we put a love that is "something active and genuine" into budget, program, and administration? Where does the journey from fear to love take us with Christian education, questions on the arms race, ministry in our hometowns, and nurturing our own? Where are we going and what will our future be?

The power to imagine what kind of congregations we can become taps the power of hope and newness. Think, if you will, about a peacemaking congregation where God's will for justice is a shared vision. How would a newcomer know this to be a peacemaking congregation? What could be observed, felt, and understood that would convey to the stranger that that is a community of justice where people are pursuers of peace?

Given the question, five minutes, a marker, and some newsprint, I have found that people—whose concept of peacemaking in the congregation had been limited to simply a committee or project—are able to articulate clearly many of the elements of what would distinguish a peacemaking congregation. Attributes of values, skills, attitudes, and program begin to surface, and as the list grows, a mosaic emerges that points far beyond a study series or forum on arms control, though certainly including them.

My sense is that too often we have limited what we can do in peacemaking because we have limited our thinking and have not defined the mission. Having a vision of what we understand the peacemaking mission to be is the first step to finding ways to infuse it into the life and ministry of the congregation. If peacemaking is to be central to the faith, what do we mean by this? What is the vision and how is it to be realized?

The Vision and Mission

Daily we see the evidence that fear evokes violence and that violence most assuredly evokes fear. This seemingly endless cycle of brokenness spirals outward through words, systems, and the use of force. But God, who is the author of true peace and security, is an active God, delivering people from their fear, creating and renewing the sense of wholeness and harmony.

Congregations who would be faithful to our God who delivers, creates, and renews, are called to restore true security in this troubled world by lessening fear and defensiveness. Therefore, the vision and mission of the peacemaking congregation might read:

We have been blessed with God's peace through forgiveness and grace. It is in this certainty that we seek to honor God's reign through spiritual wholeness and caring relationships, working for justice and a world at peace.

As a peacemaking congregation we believe God calls us to a ministry of hope through the work of love,

— breaking the cycles of brokenness and violence by addressing conditions that breed fear and defensiveness in the spiritual life, in relationships, the social order, and global community, and

— living the values that nurture authentic security, wholeness, and reconciliation through our deeds, sensitivities, and systems.

With this vision and mission, peacemaking that seemed "immense and simply impossible to handle," according to one priest, becomes a ministry that we can determine and for which we can plan.

Goals for a Peacemaking Ministry

Strategic planning takes place in most arenas of serious endeavor, whether it be a business, a school district, or a government agency. It is done to bring focus and effectiveness to a mission statement, and goal setting is part of the process. We who must wed budget and program to gospel values and a vision of peacemaking would do well to formulate our goals for acting on the mission. By establishing goals for this ministry, peacemaking can become purposeful about breaking the cycles of fear and living *shalom* values. Goals for a congregation's peacemaking ministry might be:

1. *In the spiritual life of the congregation:*

— minister to the spiritually broken whose lives reveal fear, guilt, or despair;

— nurture a spiritual life that is rooted in God's redeeming and gracious love, affirming

the importance of prayer in disarming the heart;
the Lord's Table as a global table where we celebrate with others our community in God;
Christ's ministry of suffering love to the poor and the powerless;
spiritual discernment for discovering faithful responses to our times.

2. *The life of relationships within the congregation:*

— be present to those in the congregation whose lives reveal a sense of being in crisis, unloved, devalued, lonely, or threatened;

— be a community of faith where the sense of being loved and belonging is real. Live and nurture values of interdependence, vulnerability, truth, and compassion. (See pages 45–46.)

3. *In relationship to the social order and the global community:*

— live the values of courage, righteous anger, compassion, and hopefulness (pp. 45-46) through solidarity with the victims in the areas of domestic justice, global justice, and human rights. Share in efforts to reduce militarism, reverse the arms race, and protect the earth;

— affirm global community by living out the values of nonviolent conflict resolution, shared decision-making, conserving and sharing, economic and racial justice, pluralism and inclusiveness. Seek to live and nurture the values of nonviolence.

Loving Leadership

The vision, mission, and goals provide a blueprint for the congregation. In and of themselves they are only words; albeit words that are helpful for giving direction and cohesiveness to action. If peacemaking is to become a consistent aspect of the life of the congregation, it will take leadership to breathe life into the mission. Leadership, both clergy and laity, will give peacemaking a "home" in the congregation through budget and authorization, planning, organization, and program—all the institutional valuing that we accord to those things we take seriously.

The paradox is that while leadership is required for these institutional processes for peacemaking, it cannot be leadership that insists, proceeding autocratically with pronouncements that say in essence "You will be a peacemaking congregation, or else!" Rather, servant leadership is required—leadership where power is centered within instead of being imposed from without. This lifestyle of leadership has as its role model the servant leadership of Jesus, who bathed the feet of his disciples.

Church leadership that leads in this mode is leadership that is spiritually secure and disarmed of heart. It is leadership that lives *shalom* values by modeling trust and vulnerability, valuing truth and integrity. It does not coerce; it welcomes collaboration, negotiation, diversity, and honesty in arriving at a course of action. It understands that conflict is not inherently bad; that instead, conflict that respects people and that allows for differing points of view can be the course to a better relationship. Servant leadership provides direction for peacemaking and justice seeking in ways that are lived out in day-to-day ministry. Taking courage from Christ's example, it is not intimidated by the values of the marketplace; it is able to say No to that which is expedient or that compromises the commandment to love.

Finally, servant leadership does not dominate or manipulate by means of guilt. It invites, affirms, respects, and listens, evoking the gifts of others. In short, servant leadership is loving leadership that seeks to live the vision of peacemaking. Blessed is the congregation that has such for leaders, for it is leadership that multiplies.

"*I may be able to speak the languages of men and even of angels, but if I have no love, my speech is no more than a noisy gong or a clanging bell. I may have the gift of inspired preaching; I may have all knowledge and understand all secrets; I may have all the faith needed to move mountains—but if I have no love, I am nothing. . . . Love is patient and kind; it is not jealous or conceited or proud; love is not ill-mannered or selfish or irritable; love does not keep a record of wrongs; love is not happy with evil, but is happy with the truth. Love never gives up; and its faith, hope, and patience never fail*" (1 Corinthians 13:1-2, 4-7).

12

The Warp and Woof of Peacemaking in the Congregation

In weaving a fine piece of wool, the series of yarns that extend lengthwise at intervals on the loom is called the warp. The thread that is worked back and forth across the loom is called the woof. It is woven over and under the warp, time after time, until finally the warp and woof come together in a single piece of cloth. Warp and woof are separate threads no more; they are a new entity in which their individual qualities fuse to bring forth pattern, color, and texture.

In imagining how to bring peacemaking into fullness within the congregation, it helps to think about the warp and woof, with peacemaking's vision as the fabric to be woven—the vision that seeks to honor God's reign through spiritual wholeness, caring relationships, a nation of justice, and a world at peace.

The warp of the congregation's loom presents a framework for its peacemaking. It consists of all those functions of ministry that give shape and meaning to the life of the congregation. It includes:

— worship
— nurturing of community
— study and discernment
— authorization
— empowerment

— institutional lifestyle
— political and social witness

The woof of this "peaceweaving" is the thread of mission that seeks to lessen fear, restore security, and live the *shalom* values through deeds, systems, and sensitivities. This thread of mission is woven back and forth over the various functions of ministry so that peacemaking becomes a part of the fabric of the congregation's life. The question is always asked: How can we weave the mission of peacemaking and justice seeking into the day-to-day functions of ministry?

These functions of ministry often overlap or complement each other. By way of a very simple example, the church council of a local church calls a meeting of the congregation to review and vote on a recommendation for improving energy efficiency in the educational building. The meeting is preceded by a potluck supper, some singing, a reflection on a Bible reading, and prayer. Because this congregation has done advocacy on world hunger, the shared meal is celebrated simply, with the Hunger Task Force suggesting creative alternatives to the traditional overabundance of casseroles and rich desserts. In this gathering, we find these functions of ministry: worship, nurturing community, prayer and discernment, authorization, and institutional lifestyle. Woven across the functions are facets of the mission of modeling *shalom* values: stewardship of resources, hunger awareness and simple lifestyle, shared decision-making, and fellowship. All are aspects of the congregation's peacemaking.

The vision of God's will for justice and peace is interpreted in the functions of ministry by making choices concerning values, priorities, and program that give peacemaking a consistency. In whatever it is doing, the peacemaking parish seeks to be faithful to its mission of breaking the cycles of fear and defensiveness and living the values that nurture true security, wholeness, and reconciliation.

Let's look at an example of how a local church can be intentional about integrating the goals for its peacemaking into parish life. St. John's is located in a community that has experienced violence in an extended strike of the workers at a local meat processing plant. Because of the futility of violence in settling the differences, the church council has requested the parish Peace Task Force to recommend ways that the church could model an alternative of nonviolent conflict resolution for the community, making the connection with conflict in the family, congregation, community, and world. In consultation with the pastor and related church leaders, the commission draws up a twelve-month plan for using those ideas that will best mesh with the felt needs and fears of the congregation. These are some of the possibilities within the various functions:

— regularly incorporating prayers for those involved in mediating the plant's strike during Sunday worship (worship);

— holding a Bible study series on dealing with conflict[1] (study and discernment);

— sponsoring a congregational workshop for learning the skills of nonviolent conflict resolution (empowerment);

— implementing processes for conflict prevention in the staff/board/congregation relationship (institutional lifestyle);

— offering the church facility as neutral turf for mediation proceedings in the meatpackers dispute (social witness);

— receiving an offering of letters to the President, petitioning him to agree to a moratorium in testing nuclear weapons (political witness).

As we see from our examples, the possibilities for peacemaking are exciting, for by weaving the vision and goals of ministry across the functions of life in the congregation, the unique patterns of a particular congregation's peacemaking begin to appear, and it is not difficult to understand how it can become integrated.

Paul's counsel "to use our different gifts in accordance with the grace that God has given us" (Romans 12:6) takes on a new meaning. Not everyone needs to do peacemaking in the same way, but all can participate in some way; each can respect and support others in the ways they have chosen. The perfect congregation probably doesn't exist this side of the grave, and church leaders with a vision of peacemaking will also take seriously peacemaking that ministers to those within the congregation whose lives reveal brokenness or estrangement. Usually those who make themselves unlovable need loving the most. This is where trying to understand peoples' fears and defensiveness can be very important. "Do your best to preserve the unity which the Spirit gives by means of the peace that binds you together" (Ephesians 4:3).

Having said these things, let's examine those areas in the life of the congregation that give opportunities for peacemaking and justice seeking. With a shared vision, church leaders can bring to the functions the *shalom* values of wholeness, security, love, compassion, unity, and reconciliation. This is the warp and woof of peacemaking.

Worship

Worship is at the beginning and very heart of Christian peacemaking. Thornberry speaks of worship and the "work" of the liturgy as the disciplined remembering of God's great acts and the response of God's people to those acts.[2]

In the remembering we hear God's word of love, judgment, forgiveness, and grace. The readings, prayers, sacraments, homily, and music proclaim the Good News, putting us in touch with God's gifts to us of peace and the love that casts out all fear. We worship in community with others, both those present and those throughout the world, celebrating our oneness and acknowledging our common need for God's grace and reconciliation.

In worship we respond as God's people to God's gracious acts with words and songs of praise, gifts of thanksgiving, prayers of confession and intercession, and acts of rededication for bringing God's peace to others through deeds of compassion and justice.

The worship of peacemaking is not simply a preparation for activism. While it can and does move us to do other things, it is also an end in itself. Richard Watts, an author for the Presbyterian Peacemaking Program, observes that

> praying for enemies is itself a work of peacemaking. Laying our brokenness before God for healing is itself peacemaking. Joining hands around the Lord's Table with neighbors we don't like too much is itself peacemaking. Renewing our allegiance to Jesus Christ as Lord is itself peacemaking.[3]

Watts frames the relationship of worship to Christian peacemaking by asking: What are some of the marks of authentic worship for peacemakers? He notes that in authentic peacemaking worship, a number of things occur:

— *We reclaim our true identity*, distancing ourselves from all human institutions that would claim our ultimate loyalty. We are first of all children of God through Jesus Christ. Jesus is Lord; Caesar isn't. Our security rests in the certainty of God's grace, not in nuclear weapons.

— *We name names* wherever there is conflict, injustice, and violence in human life, replacing bland generalities with specific naming of our needs for God's peace. (Instead of praying "for all the world's suffering children," we pray for the children of South Africa being held in detention centers.)

— *We pray for enemies* as we disavow tribal deities and honor the God of all nations. We also pray for nearby personal enemies whom we find hard to forgive.

— *We admit our complicity* in injustice and violence, confessing that we and ours are sometimes part of the problem.

— *We focus on a vision*, inviting others to rekindle faith in God, who intends a future for this planet marked by such blessings as good health, a secure life, an end to hunger, and the reconciliation of people to each other and to their Creator.

— Finally, for many, *peacemaking worship centers in the Lord's Supper*, where we confess our sin and brokenness, reunite with our brothers and sisters in faith, accept God's reconciling love, and receive Christ's blessing, "Peace be with you. As the Father sent me, so I send you" (John 20:21).[4]

Watts' discussion makes it clear that peacemaking's worship is not a matter of putting together all the Bible verses, songs, and readings we can find that talk about peace. For, as Watts wisely observes, people bring to the hour of worship personal problems, family needs, doubts, gratitude, the quest for meaning—things that are often ignored in a single-issue service. R. Blair Moffett counsels that while some services may focus on a particular challenge of peacemaking, peacemaking can't be relegated to a special day any more than can joy or love or thanksgiving.[5] Fidelity to the lectionary and the church year will assure a pastor of countless opportunities to incorporate God's will for justice and righteousness into the planning of the sermons, hymns, and special offerings.

Some things to consider in planning authentic peacemaking worship include the following:[6]

— Prayers should reflect societal hurts and aspirations as well as individual or congregational concerns. Prayers for peace should name names, places, and situations.

— A sharing of concerns from the people before the pastoral prayer nurtures peacemaking as people call others to join them in praying for a specific person, injustice, or concern.

— Inclusive language and sermons that reflect a global perspective demonstrate that God is clearly the God of all nations and of the whole human family. For ministry to be faithful it must express God's concern for the whole earth and all its peoples.

— Moments of silence following the sermon will allow people the space to consider the meaning of this reflection upon Scripture for their own lives.

— "Passing the Peace" with the greeting, "The peace of Christ be with you" often precedes the Lord's Supper. This ancient church custom recognizes God's gift of grace and symbolizes our reconciliation. A congregation that shares in this fellowship is a company of peacemakers, participating in the gift of God's healing love. (1 John 1:7)

— Reclaiming and reinterpreting the forms of worship is part of the work of peacemaking, for sometimes liturgical terms can become so commonplace that we lose sight of their significance. Each time we celebrate baptism, for example, we affirm that God has made peace with us, reconciling us through Jesus Christ. The relationship of this to our peacemaking needs to be affirmed from time to time.

— Regular moments of concern during the worship service will afford church leaders the opportunity to lift up special peace and justice needs with opportunities for action by the congregation.

— Having an offering of letters is a meaningful follow-up to a specific peace and justice concern. With stamps, pens, and stationery available in the narthex, members can write their letters to express concern or advocate legislative action to national leaders. The letters are received as an offering during the worship service.

— The music of worship can enable the work for justice and peace. With peacemaking in mind, many familiar hymns take on new meaning. The congregation can be invited to be open to this. The choir, too, is a source of the music of peace.

— Finally, prayer should not be confined to the sanctuary. Given a vision of God's peacemaking taking place in all aspects of church life, the peacemaking congregation will incorporate moments of prayer and reflection at the beginning of all church meetings and endeavors. Prayers of expectation will open the hearts of the people to the works of the Spirit.

Nurturing Community

"*All the believers continued together in close fellowship and shared their belongings with one another. They would sell their property and possessions, and distribute the money among all, according to what each needed. Day after day they met as a group in the Temple, and they had their meals together in their homes, eating with glad and humble hearts, praising God, and enjoying the good will of all the people. And everyday the Lord added to their group those who were being saved*" (Acts 2:44-47).

What an incredible experience it must have been to be an early Christian! We are told the people were of one heart, sharing all that they had with each other and selling their possessions to help those in need. What's more, daily they came together at the temple and ate in each other's homes. These were glad folks, alive to their love of God, enjoying the respect of others. These were a people of community. The significance of their life together was confirmed as regularly they added to their numbers. All this occurred, mind you, without workshops on community-building, curricula on economic justice, or seminars on evangelism. Incredible, indeed!

Because community is inherent to God's nature of love and reconciliation, proclaimed in the life of Jesus and given unique expression in the early church, it is a heritage to be cherished, cared for, and constantly renewed. No one needs to be reminded of the profound differences between life for the Christians of Palestine in the first century and life in the United States as we approach the year 2000. The complexities of this new age called postmodernity make for some critical differences in the way

Christians experience community. But the essence of community is not bound to a single time and place; through the witness of the early church we are given a model for peacemaking through community for congregations of today.

Let us examine five important elements of their model.

1. Fellowship

The early Christians knew they were loved and that they belonged. They found strength and security in God's love and in their fellowship with each other. Safe in that love, they became fearless, not only selling their possessions but some even risking arrest and death to bring the Good News to others.

Their model of *agape* love has special meaning for churches in this high tech nuclear age. Today there is an urgent need for congregations to be communities of faith where people feel God's *shalom* by being valued, accepted, and treated as friends. The close fellowship described in Acts must have shown itself in many ways; it should go without saying that it included greeting, touching, and making eye contact. But we who would be fearless are often afraid of even greeting the stranger sitting next to us in the pew, and we avoid the eyes of one struggling with family chaos because of our feelings of inadequacy. The fear of the Imperfect Self even strikes us in the sanctuary. In a workshop I gave on peacemaking, a woman commented that it was difficult for some people to pass the peace because the act of touching was somehow threatening. A man who had belonged to the church for years said he never shook hands with anyone at church "because I find it hard to let down my guard." Even in the most elementary ways we need to encourage members to feel secure enough in God's gracious love to extend warmth and caring to others in the fellowship and to those who are visitors.

The fellowship of community is also known in the ways we come together. In planning our meetings, organizations, and shared meals, we can nurture the possibilities for fellowship by considering questions such as these:

— How are newcomers identified, acknowledged, and invited to participate?

— How can we encourage people to mix and to learn something new about people seated near them?

— How can we bring a feeling of collective joy and cohesiveness to an event or meeting?

— Do we plan in ways that are sensitive to varied family structures, diverse economic situations, and different age groups?

— In planning meetings and events, do we consider the stressful demands on the time of single parents and two-income families?

2. Compassion

The early Christians invested in community to the point of selling their possessions and distributing the money according to need. It is hard to imagine this kind of response to economic disparity in most churches today, although it still can be found in some pentecostal churches and religious communities ministering to the poor in the cities. Those of us electing house payments, tuition costs, and creature comforts are challenged by the example of the early Christians to a deeper level of sacrificial giving so that ministries done through our parish for those with special needs can flourish.

Solidarity is a word for home turf, too. The fellowship of a community is also about being present to those in the congregation who are in crisis, lonely, or in special need, by responding in concrete and specific ways. Our gifts to discretionary funds can help with someone of our congregation needing special counseling or a wheelchair, or perhaps a single parent coping with an emergency. The offer for child care, the delivery of a relative to the airport, or the time to simply listen are examples of how the community cares about its own. Some of the responses can and should be organized through committees, but all caring cannot be delegated if we are to be sincere about community. What skills can we share with others?

3. Participation

The fellowship of the early church is also a model in participation. Community is enriched when work and planning are shared and when there is an element of change in the roles. We can get so locked into asking the same people to take the same responsibilities, often because they do them well, that we lose sight of how the habit not only denies us the discovery of new talents, but it also solidifies groups and arrangements. When participation and responsibility in the various jobs of a congregation become predictable, a church's fellowship is at risk; it can become instead a closed fellowship.

This can have damaging affects on the way a church handles conflict. Ron Kraybill, director of the Mennonite Conciliation Service and consultant to congregations in conflict, speaks of "the cross-stitching effect of groups" on conflict. In churches where networks and roles overlap and change, the bonds of friendship and knowledge bring healthy dimensions to differences, so that, properly managed, the differences can bring new meaning and actually foster new possibilities. But in parishes where groups and networks are entrenched or solidified, conflict and differences can become threatening and divisive, with the sense of community being seriously jeopardized.[7]

4. Communication

The fact that the early Christians met daily tells us that, among other things, they valued good communication. Today, while we cannot meet daily, the avenues for good communication are open to us and their use is imperative. Several levels of communication are significant for nurturing community in a peacemaking congregation:

— Church newsletters, the reporting of church business and decisions, and news from the denomination or archdiocese, are important mechanisms for general information and accountability. Disseminating this type of information accords respect and accountability to those supporting the program and ministry of the church.

— The opportunity for church members to offer opinions and feedback to church leaders will improve participation in the church's ministry and program. A mark of servant leadership, be it clergy or laity, is the security to seek and value this type of information. Having processes in place and in use for evaluation and feedback is an aid to conflict prevention. Leadership that blocks this type of communication is acting at cross purposes with peacemaking.

— The clergy and lay leaders of the congregation need to be able to be honest and direct with the members about items of concern, whether they be of ministry, program, or business. The truth spoken in love must have been a precept of those early Christians who met together daily. May we benefit from their example.

5. Worship and Breaking Bread

Worshiping and eating together were synonymous with community for the early Christians; they engaged in both acts together daily. Today some elements of each continue to enrich our sense of loving and belonging whenever we come together for business, study, or celebration. Weekly corporate worship and the celebration of the Lord's Supper are the means for giving these times for Christian community their most tangible expression.

"*They spent their time in learning from the apostles, taking part in the fellowship, and sharing in the fellowship meals and the prayers*" (Acts 2:42).

Study and Discernment

A section of *Peacemaking: The Believers' Calling*, a policy paper of the United Presbyterian Church (U.S.A.), reads, "The church must discern the signs of the times in light of what the Spirit is revealing. . . . We are at a turning point . . . faced with the decision either to serve the Rule of God or to side with the powers of death through our complacency and silence." This statement and recent pastoral letters by other denominations call upon congregations to study and reflect on the Scriptures and contemporary realities in order to discover God's will for us.

A parish's understanding of God determines its discernment of the times and the way it responds. The questions that must be honestly considered are these: Are we a congregation that uses God primarily as a custodian for our personal needs? Are we a congregation that seeks to manage God as the protector of our interests? Or, as a worshiping community, do we believe that God is free, acting in human history? What is our claim?

One can learn something about how a congregation answers these questions by reading the schedules in the Sunday bulletin or the monthly newsletter. Sometimes it is a lack of balance in the activities that gives clues to the answer. In a church where the majority of the activities and concerns have to do with weddings, funerals, bazaars, softball games, and wine and cheese parties to the exclusion of much else, one could conclude that God is perceived as One who simply blesses and comforts, sanctioning what would probably be happening anyway, whether it be with civil authorities, service clubs, or the local sports league. The fellowship in such a parish can be club-like, and, while the people may indeed have fun and enjoy belonging, God's will for justice and compassion has little to do with determining the agenda. There appears to be little or no desire to inquire or move things out of the comfort zone, and evangelism is almost a foreign word because the Good News may mean little more than that the church has met its budget. Through its monthly track record, this parish answers Yes to the first question: Are we a congregation that uses God primarily as a custodian for our personal needs?

What about the question of managing God for our own gain? How do we answer? This is the congregation that prays to God as the protector of interests, and these are often patriotic interests. In the minds of the people, God has been domesticated for serving national interests, and nuclear weapons may well be appreciated as an extension of God's will to "maintain the peace." Some would see this kind of peace as the imposed peace of Caesar's Rome, the *pax Romana*. This is often a comfortable church where servanthood, inclusiveness, and economic justice are not understood to be elements of the Good News. As in the first parish, there can be a strong sense of belonging. But unlike the first, study and prayer *are* priorities, with discernment including analysis by a religion that has been nationalized and in which God is seen as the guardian in the country's moral and military combat with "godless and evil nations." The Armageddon of Revelation 16 may be interpreted as a time of nuclear holocaust from which only "Christian nations" will be delivered for the second coming of Christ. Or, if not that explicit, there is still a strong moral and religious justification for this nation, whose pledge states "under God," to have a first-strike nuclear policy. Confession and repentance are regarded as only individual matters.

The third congregation has yet another view of God determining the nature of its worship, fellowship, and the way it uses its time to act on its mission. This congregation's understanding of God is that of Yahweh, as God was revealed to Moses, "I am who I am" (Exodus 3:14). Yahweh is free: "I will be what I will be," not used, managed, domesticated, or cast into a gendered mold. God is known as compassionate, entering into the suffering of the people: "I know all about their sufferings, and so I have come down to rescue them from the Egyptians. . . . I have indeed heard the cry of my people" (Exodus 3:7, 9). This congregation understands its mission to be servant church of the Servant Lord in a ministry of compassion, justice, and reconciliation. Furthermore, it remembers that God is the same Yahweh that loved all people, including Israel's enemies. (In an ancient Jewish commentary on Exodus 15, the Lord God silences the women's celebration over the Egyptian army's disaster in the Red Sea, crying out, "You rejoice as my children are dying? They, too, are mine."[8]) This congregation understands God's love to be present to all people, regardless of nationality, ethnicity, politics, or human boundaries. There is a keen sense here of God's grace and of a God who "so loved the world. . . . "

These three understandings of the nature of God have everything to do with how a congregation discerns the times and, therefore, with establishing the mission and agenda for what it does and why it does what it does. The peacemaking congregation, hearing the cry of God's people, asks, "Why are things the way they are? Do they have to be this way? How are we, as people of faith, called to respond?" To help bring peace with justice to human institutions and the nations of the world, it engages in discernment that is both biblically and theologically informed, as well as honest to the context of today's experiences. Analysis of the social order cannot be ignored.

A biblically informed social analysis includes much of the same data as secular efforts in probing causes and assessing consequences in social problems, as well as identifying the linkages and roles of those affected and involved. However, in the peacemaking congregation, analysis also includes theological reflection and faith-based planning for change. The discernment process includes:

—*awareness of the experiences of people*, especially the poor and oppressed, and of how they are responding to their realities;

—*social analysis of these experiences*, making structural connections between such things as political power, economics, natural resources, and history;

—*theological reflection on the experiences* of the people and social analysis, with the word of God raising new questions, and suggesting new insights and responses;

—*faith-based planning to respond*, asking, "What does our faith call us to do and how might we respond most effectively?"[9]

This is done in the belief that the God who was involved with the people of biblical times is the same God who is involved with people today, and the biblical story will help to discern something of God's activity in today's events. Believing that God is indeed the free Yahweh who hears the cry of the suffering and enters into human history, the peacemaking congregation, through prayer and discernment, seeks to discover God's intention for it, and also it discerns how to respond. It seeks to work with God to create a new experience.

This view of an active and compassionate God whose will is justice will furnish the pastor, church council, board of Christian education, and the parish organizations with much grist for the mill in determining faithful responses to the times. Study and discernment will be part of the life of the church. They will enrich worship, fellowship, and organizational life. And they will indeed be reflected in the projects and programs announced in the church bulletin and discussed in the newsletter.

One might wonder about practical approaches that assist in the process of linking faith with daily living. McGinnis discusses the process of people moving from awareness to faith-based action on social concerns as a process requiring the development of compassion. He identifies four elements for developing the capacity for compassion.[10] Being aware of these elements can help us in our planning. They include people:

(1) being touched by the lives and experiences of the victims of injustice, which shifts perception from faceless statistics to real people in real situations. (See pages 59–60 for possibilities in the congregation.)

(2) being touched by the witness of people who are advocates for justice. Inviting them to speak, visiting their workplaces, or volunteering provides inspiration and new insights.

(3) interpreting the work for peace and justice as a call, made audible through Scripture, the presence of Christ in others, and by the Spirit.

(4) being supported and challenged by a small, trusting community of faith with which to study, share, pray, and plan action.

Meanwhile, back at the Church of New Beginnings, Hometown, U.S.A., what are some ways for encouraging prayer, study, and discernment in the existing program? These are just a few of many possibilities:

— Plan a study and discernment series using your denomination's pastoral letter or pronouncement on peace and justice. People can be reminded that these papers are not intended as the church speaking for them, but rather they are a way for the church to talk with its people about matters of faith. Give careful thought to leadership and process.

— Encourage an active prayer life and have personal meditation resources available that have justice values and a global perspective. Check with your denomination. (Other possibilities: Pax Christi USA, 348 E. 10th St., Erie, PA 16503 and the annual daily scripture readings of Biblical Witness to Peacemaking from Presbyterian Distribution Service, 475 Riverside Dr., #905, New York, NY 10115)

— Issue an invitation to those interested in focusing on a vision for your congregation's peacemaking and justice seeking to participate in a six-week prayer and study group. Offer a selection of study aids and invite those participating to select one to be used.

— Use the model of awareness, analysis, reflection, and planning to discern a response by your congregation to a local concern: e.g., toxic waste disposal, the closing of a clinic, farm families in crisis.

— Introduce the principles of study and discernment to the youth. Studying and reflecting on the systemic causes of hunger could be part of an extended project in which both deeds of mercy and deeds of justice were utilized.[11]

— Integrate reflection and discernment into the process of making major decisions within the various church boards. It is important that the church, at committee level and board level, maintain an intentional faith and justice link with the business at hand.

To worship, study, struggle, and celebrate in the spirit of community is the essence of our life together. When done in the spirit of faithfulness to the God of justice and love, God's Spirit will bring forth from us the works of peace.

Warp and woof, vision and mission, values and function—these are ways for a congregation to think about peacemaking so that "the vastness and impossibility of the task" are forever removed. We have begun our peaceweaving by considering three of the threads comprising the warp of the congregation's peacemaking loom. Beginning with worship, nurturing community, and study and discernment, we have considered faithfulness to God's will for *shalom* in these functions of church life. Patterns and texture begin to appear that will come into their own as we continue.

(The chart on page 111 depicts how the vision and mission of a congregation's peacemaking flows through the leadership and into the life of the congregation through the functions of ministry, resulting in deeds of justice, peace, and reconciliation.)

The Peacemaking Congregation

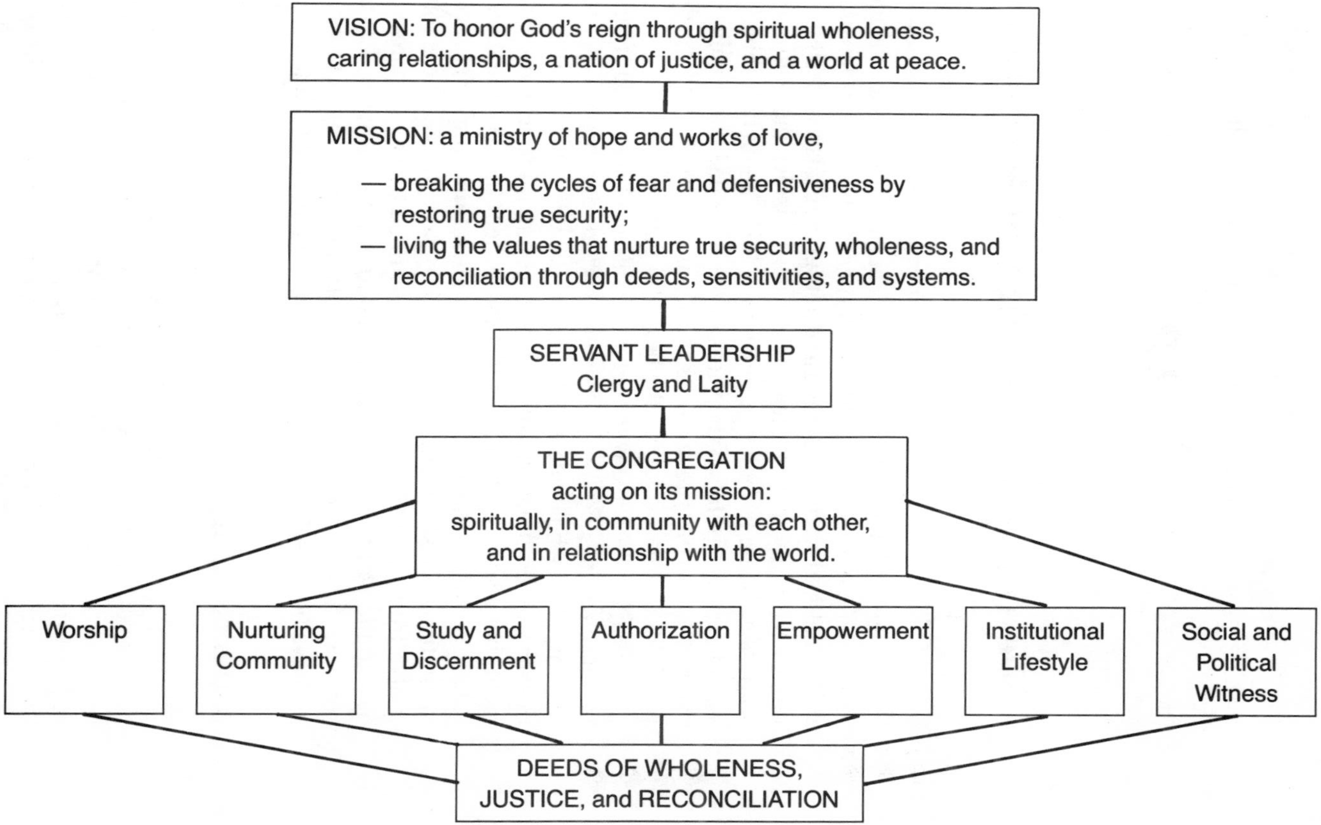

VISION: To honor God's reign through spiritual wholeness, caring relationships, a nation of justice, and a world at peace.
MISSION: a ministry of hope and works of love,
— breaking the cycles of fear and defensiveness by restoring true security;
— living the values that nurture true security, wholeness, and reconciliation through deeds, sensitivities, and systems.
SERVANT LEADERSHIP
Clergy and Laity
THE CONGREGATION
acting on its mission:
spiritually, in community with each other, and in relationship with the world.
Worship
Nurturing Community
Study and Discernment
Authorization
Empowerment
Institutional Lifestyle
Social and Political Witness
DEEDS OF WHOLENESS, JUSTICE, and RECONCILIATION

13

Weaving a Completed Pattern

On the wall above my desk hangs a beautifully woven Navajo rug—rich colors of red, gold, green, and brown woven across a wheat-colored warp. The pattern, exciting in its classic design, is one of harmony and wholeness. As we consider the warp and woof of a congregation's peacemaking, I think about how this rug would appear if some of the yarns of the warp had been omitted. Were this so, the rug would have been narrower, limiting the possibilities for developing the beautiful pattern.

It is much the same with weaving a full and harmonious fabric of peacemaking. For the pattern and texture of a parish's peacemaking to be whole and authentic, we need to consider not only the threads or functions of worship, community, and discernment, but also other functions that implement the congregation's values of faith—the functions of authorization, empowerment, institutional lifestyle, and political and social witness. These four evolve from the first three, being determined by our responsiveness to the word and *agape* love, and to our discernment. Let us consider them as we seek to bring unity and faithfulness to what we have been called to do and who we have been called to be.

Authorization

"Peacemaking needs strong support from the minister and it needs an official home in church structure." This single sentence from the pastor of a United Church of Christ congregation with an active peace and justice task force says succinctly what is needed for peacemaking to become central and integrated in the life of a congregation: pastoral support and authorization by the church's governing body. It is through these that peacemaking can move from being the consuming concern of a faithful few to a priority that has ownership and institutional valuing with a budget.

To the peacemaker who wonders what act of God might be needed to bring this about, another minister, Rev. Brad Kent of St. Louis, brings some helpful counsel. Kent, who chairs the Committee on Peacemaking for the Synod of MidAmerica of the Presbyterian Church (U.S.A.), presented this wisdom on authorization at a seminar sponsored by the Institute for Peace and Justice at Eden Theological Seminary:

Beginning with Yourself

Just as we sing "Let it begin with me," one must begin with oneself in obtaining an official home for the parish's peacemaking, making peacemaking a priority rather than one of ten other things. It is a vocation of discipleship with the attending costs. Be willing to accept hostility and frustration. Remember that in peacemaking the end dictates the means; *do* peacemaking as you work toward your goal of peacemaking (as opposed to using terrorism to combat terrorism.) Be reconciling and avoid labeling people or putting them down. Remember that you cannot impose your agenda on others. The issues and felt needs of your congregation will emerge; attend to them.

Keep the biblical and theological basis for peacemaking foremost when discussing it with others in the congregation. By doing this, peacemaking will not get sidetracked as others are called to consider the claim of the gospel on their lives.

Talking to the Pastor

In the process of seeking authorization and organization for your church's peacemaking, the pastor needs to be in on the ground level. He or she will give you an invaluable perspective on the possibilities, knowing the diversity and orientation of the people as only a pastor can.

Do everything in consultation with the pastor; pastors don't need or like big surprises. Besides expressing your own hopes and concerns, find out where he or she is on things. What frightens or worries your pastor? What makes her or him feel good? What areas of peacemaking interest her? In what areas could he be supportive?

Remember that you are not in the pastor's office to sell a program. You are there to build on things that are already taking place. Identify those things that are already going on in the congregation that are authentic peacemaking. Explain that your hope is for engaging the church council in order to systematize and build on what is already being done by giving it an official church home, with authorization, support, and accountability.

Talking to the Governing Body

Once again, keeping the biblical and theological basis for peacemaking as a primary consideration, meet with the parish council, reviewing the authentic peacemaking that is already taking place. Ask that peacemaking be given (1) a *place* in the church's structure of authorization, support, and accountability, and (2) a *form of organization* with the appointment of a task force directly accountable to the council if possible.

Request a job description for the task force, preparing some suggestions, which state (1) a purpose that is biblically and theologically grounded, (2) goals and objectives, (3) a clear idea of structure, stating who makes up the task force, how long they serve, and how they are chosen, and (4) specifics on accountability, evaluation, and reporting.

For peacemaking to become integrated into the total life of the church, the task force should be representative of the congregation, not "loaded" ideologically. Kent notes that strategically it is important to get males involved in order to get beyond the mindset that "peace is a women's concern." Report to the council *regularly*, reviewing the work that is underway, as well as sharing what the denomination is doing and how your church is a part of the ongoing work of the denomination.

Going to the Congregation

Prepare a bulletin board display with pictures and examples of peacemaking at the Church of New Beginnings, affirming and celebrating those things already underway. The people will be happy to know that they are already engaged in peacemaking to an extent that they may not have realized.

Start publicizing what has happened with the church council. *Report regularly* in the church newsletter, giving the whole range of peacemaking news, including that of the denomination, showing how it is being integrated into the life of the church.

Prayer is essential. Your efforts and the efforts of the pastor, council, and the task force need divine linkage. Begin all peacemaking meetings and activities with prayer, which in essence should be all church meetings and activities, and close with prayer. Pray with expectancy.

Lessons Learned[1]

Rarely do our efforts proceed without problems, but we can learn from our mistakes and the experiences of others. These are some examples:

— "We made the mistake of assuming that people would welcome and participate in peacemaking activities without first having a personal, spiritual sense of peacemaking." (Presbyterian, Missouri)

— "The peacemaking-justice ministry has been given the same dignity as our other ministries. In any parish this work *must* be in the same level as other work, i.e., educational, liturgy, councils, etc." (Roman Catholic, Arizona)

— "We've learned it was a false assumption to believe that peace can be discussed, studied, and in sermons without noticeable discord. We have learned to approach the subject with love and patience." (United Church of Christ, Michigan)

— "When warriors join your peace effort, it gets co-opted." (Lutheran, Missouri)

— "We underestimated the concern and support that are here." (United Church of Christ, Missouri)

— "I thought I was the only one who interpreted God's Word to be one of peace and justice. I've found there are others here, just as afraid as I am at times. We find strength in each other." (Roman Catholic, Illinois)

— "We often get into the trap of decrying the lack of action/involvement of others in order to be able to affirm our own. Give credit to the grace that enables you—and let your primary concern be that of what you yourself have 'done or left undone' and make no judgment of others. Affirm, affirm, affirm!" (Episcopal, Missouri)

Empowerment

We church folk have a tendency to dull the impact of the language of faith by using good words too often. Empowerment, one such word, is used often in policy and pronouncements, but the frequency of its use does not guarantee follow-through. If we are to use this word in our peacemaking, it is important that we use it with care and integrity.

What does it mean for empowerment to be a function of a church's ministry and for what are we empowering? Put simply, to empower is to make it possible to do something. As a function of Christian peacemaking, empowerment has to do with tapping the passion, will, and commitment that people feel about peace, justice, and reconciliation, by providing knowledge, skills, and support that will enable them to act with effectiveness. We have a mission to lessen fear by restoring true security and to live the values that nurture true security, wholeness, and reconciliation. Enabling people to discover and effectively use the power within them to act on this mission will help to put to rest destructive myths that are etched like graffiti into public consciousness: "In conflict someone wins and someone loses," "I can't make any difference," "War is inevitable," or "I don't know enough to challenge the experts." Action that is born of love, nurtured by knowledge, and trained for effectiveness is a testimony of hope.

Opportunities to "think globally and act locally" can be inherent to empowerment. When we teach skills in nonviolent conflict resolution in the family or workplace, for example, linkages can be made with nonviolent conflict resolution between nations. With church leadership that has a world view, in many cases the skills and knowledge that empower people for personal and interpersonal justice and reconciliation can be used as a springboard to contexts of institutions, communities, and nations.

What might be some specific ways the Church of New Beginnings could empower its people to break the cycles of fear and conflict and live the values that nurture wholeness, justice, peace, and reconciliation? Each parish is the best judge of its needs as well as its fears and gifts, but it is important to be intentional about assessing these needs and then deciding on priorities and developing a plan. The following are a sampling of ways peacemaking can be done through empowerment for the mission:

1. Provide training for developing and using good verbal communication skills. Being able to listen and to talk about needs and wants in ways that are both caring and assertive is a skill of peacemaking.

2. Form support groups for people dealing with special needs. Single parenting, coping with unemployment, being "parents" to aged parents, resolving the moral conflicts of defense-related jobs, or learning to live better with less are examples of areas where the company of others can be a strengthening agent.

3. Offer church-wide training in conflict resolution. Though often denied, conflict and controversy are present in all relationships and institutions. Training in the prevention and resolution of conflict has value for the life of the congregation, the family, the workplace, and the nation.

"Congregations often avoid or deny conflict because they fear it," notes Ron Kraybill of the Mennonite Conciliation Service. Instead they adopt a "wait, hope, and pray" approach, which often results in people withdrawing from participation or leaving the church. Kraybill notes that responding to conflict in positive ways is central to the vitality of the parish.

Conflict need not be a win/lose situation, either personally or globally. Conflict management styles differ with people and situations. The manner in which both the issues and the people of the conflict are valued helps to determine a healthy or unhealthy style. Excellent resources to aid churches in conflict prevention are available.[2]

4. Equip the parents and their small children to grow as peacemaking families. The Parenting for Peace and Justice Network is a source of creative aids, ideas, and programs to help parents and parishes incorporate justice and peace values into church and family living. Countering materialism, dealing with violence, and developing healthy racial attitudes are a few of the areas included.[3]

5. Teach cooperation, interdependence, and respect for others through the toys, books, and games used in the life of the parish. Guns and war toys of any sort have no place in the nursery or preschool of a peacemaking congregation.[4] Books should

portray an appreciation for people of other colors and cultures. With the youth, use some of the new noncompetitive games that foster cooperation and interdependence.[5]

6. Support the youth of the congregation in making informed and faith-based decisions on military service. Recruiters and commercials promote the so-called "personal benefits" without discussing the human and moral costs of life in the military. Balance this input with information and counsel that considers faith, morality, and alternatives. If youth leaders are not grounded in this, seek outside help. Be intentional about it; being honest with our youth about the waging of war has too often been abdicated by the local church.[6]

7. Develop the congregation's world view. Communicate to both adults and children that differences are to be valued rather than feared, and teach about the social and economic realities of Third World nations. This can be facilitated in a variety of ways, including the pulpit, church school, church library, visuals in the halls, talks by missionaries and social justice advocates, pairing projects with sister congregations in other countries, and the sale of crafts from Third World cooperatives enabling education about the countries producing the crafts.[7]

8. Sponsor a session on Advocacy Know-how to assist members of the congregation in expressing their justice concerns through effective letter writing, meeting with legislators, and networking with others. Write an article for the church newsletter on effective legislative letter writing, giving names and addresses of senators and representatives.

9. Provide members the support of information and counsel on matters of conscience and national policy. Acknowledging that some members may be frightened or angered by this, the peacemaking congregation supports those who are struggling with questions of conscience, such as defense-related employment, alternatives to military service, war-tax resistance, and civil disobedience.

Such is the sampling of ways to empower people to effectively respond with their peacemaking and justice seeking. Each church will need to discern what forms are appropriate to its needs in providing the people with skills, knowledge, and support for being agents of hope.

Institutional Lifestyle

"*The world and all that is in it belong to the Lord; the earth and all who live on it are his*" (Psalm 24:1).

Jesus sometimes spoke of stewards, those who manage the affairs of large households. The word "stewardship" in the context of the faith acknowledges our relationship to God's household. God is the head of it, blessing us with life, time, and a place to live out our lives. As stewards, we are accountable; the way we treat the household of creation and those inhabiting it reveals our treasure (Matthew 6:21). What we do with our resources of time, money, and abilities speaks of who or what we worship.

Faithful stewardship is the bedrock for a congregation's peacemaking. Through specific choices in managing the parish household, we can bring integrity to the church's mission of nurturing people and doing justice. One might envision the annual report of a congregation, listing as its assets the energy of the people, their skills, the money they have given, and the building with its grounds. *Recognizing the finiteness of a congregation's money, time, and energies, as well as the need to protect the earth's sustenance, the question that must be constantly reviewed is: How can these finite assets be faithfully used to express* shalom *values, both within and beyond the congregation?*

The question suggests that responding with integrity will require an institutional lifestyle of simplicity. A report of the Presbyterian Church (U.S.) in 1979 stated:

> We are called individually and ecclesiastically to choose a lifestyle which more nearly reflects the simplicity of Jesus' life and allows us to identify with the poor and powerless. . . . Such an altered lifestyle enables us to reconsider what we truly value in life, . . . how we invest our lives and resources. . . . In short, we are challenged to live more simply that all may simply live.[8]

The comment of a Nicaraguan pastor returning from North America puts light on the above statement: "You wouldn't believe the churches in North America. They are all luxurious. For one church there we could build fifty here." Or listen to a pastor's wife from the Philippines: "If we could only have one-fourth of some of the Mennonite church buildings for our use in the Philippines! I don't mean I want the *beauty* of those churches for our work—just the roof and the walls!"[9] (In North America, Mennonite churches are noted for their simplicity.)

The Church of New Beginnings has considered some of these matters, deciding to take a fresh look at its stewardship of energies, time, budget, and building. The people are asking: How can our use of these assets best do justice, nurture people, and protect the earth? To begin the process, the Peace Task Force is sponsoring a Day of Discernment for the congregation. Following Sunday worship and a meal together, the people will work in small groups, identifying possible ways they can conserve, share, give, spend, and invest to better reflect their mission of peacemaking. From the emerging possibilities they will select several to seriously consider for implementation.

The purpose is to check institutional drift where clarity of purpose and intention have become obscured and to bring ownership to choices and priorities. In broad strokes, what follows are some of the questions that the people will be asking themselves.

On Conserving

A Roman Catholic priest from St. Louis recently commented that an obstacle to his parish's peacemaking was too many church programs. Another said, "We need to examine how we prioritize our time and resources." In specific ways, then, how can we simplify what we do and the way we do things in order to release resources of money, time, and energies from institutional maintenance for use in nurturing people and doing justice? These are some areas to consider: meetings, the physical plant, celebrations, preparations for church-wide events, and program priorities.

How can we better "manage the household" to conserve natural resources and not do violence to the earth? How much, for example, do we depend on plastics, disposables, pesticides, and air conditioning? How might different scheduling reduce energy costs and needs for space?

On Sharing

Specifically, how can we share our facility to respond to community or broader church needs? Can space be converted to provide room for a food co-op or food pantry? Can we provide office space to a group or agency in ministry? Could our church grounds be used for community gardening? Can our educational facility be used for child or elder care? Do community organizations that contribute to wholeness need a place to meet? Could we offer our premises for sanctuary for people fleeing political oppression in Central America or South Africa?

Are there people with skills of craft, trade, or profession within our congregation that could benefit organizations that minister to the poor and powerless, either by volunteering or teaching these skills to others? A congregation in a rural area near St. Louis recently provided a crew of members to install dry wall in a house being rehabbed in East St. Louis, Illinois, for Habitat for Humanity. Accounting and computer skills, tutoring in reading, and legal services are other possibilities for this kind of stewardship.

On Giving

What do our giving patterns beyond denominational priorities reflect? Is there a balance between emergency aid, self-help, education, advocacy, and systemic change? Do we have criteria for reviewing requests? If so, can we reaffirm the criteria or do we need to revise them?

As a congregation, do we contribute resources of time and money to the work of (1) direct service organizations such as neighborhood houses, Meals on Wheels, and the Red Cross blood program; (2) drives for voter registration; (3) organized efforts on housing or economic dislocation such as farmers or people let go from industry; (4) the work for peace and social justice done by local groups and organizations?

On Spending

Do we act on the intention to support economic development by supporting small businesses and those owned by minorities, women, or the disabled? Do we seek out their bids for services or purchase church and office supplies from them? Is racial justice a criterion in decisions about contracting for repairs, maintenance, and construction?

Do we have integrity about being an equal opportunity employer in the search and hiring process for every position that is available?

On Banking and Investing

Do we have a policy for church banking that is clear about social responsibility in the bank's internal operation? A few examples include: an official policy and mechanism for the bank itself to examine questions of social responsibility; conformance with affirmative action in hiring and upgrading minority and women personnel; loan policies that include capitalization for minority and small businesses; home loans in urban areas; a program for free checking for the poor.

Are our church investments in companies that sustain and renew life with track records of ecological responsibility, justice with workers, and fairness in the marketplace? Is divesture a consideration for faithfulness?

Could we benefit from information from the Interfaith Center on Corporate Responsibility?[10] Are there local credit unions supporting neighborhood development in poor areas where we could place some of our funds? Could our building be used as collateral in helping an agency seeking a loan?

As stewards of the household, we have been entrusted with much. Much is required from those to whom much has been given; much more is required from those to whom much more is given (Luke 12:48). Thus is the journey from fear to love.

Political and Social Witness

> Peace cannot be limited to a mere absence of war, the result of an ever precarious balance of forces. No, peace is something built up day after day, in the pursuit of an order intended by God, which implies a more perfect form of justice among men and women.—Pope Paul VI[11]

> [The nuclear crisis] is a crisis of human community. . . . We urge a renewed commitment to building the institutional foundations of common security, economic justice, human rights, and environmental conservation.—Pastoral Letter, United Methodist Council of Bishops[12]

We, who come to the Lord's Table, come to a global table knowing no human or national boundaries. Each time we share in the wine and the bread we are in community with Christ and our brothers and sisters whom he loves — those near and far and in every condition of sadness, oppression, pain, or estrangement. As we partake in this meal of God's peacegiving we are reconciled with God and each other; we are renewed for peacemaking and for bringing the bread of justice to the order and structure of our world, for it is in doing justice and in working for genuine security and reconciliation that the peace church finally weaves the completed pattern.

Peacemaking through witness and prophetic action must finally occur if the church is to be faithful to the Good News. "We are called," counsel the Catholic bishops in their Pastoral Letter on War and Peace, "to move from discussion to witness and action."[13] It is virtually impossible for a congregation to enter into witness and action in a sustained and authentic way without a vision of peace and justice in the other functions of church life. But in like manner, without political and social engagement the church's peacemaking lacks unity and wholeness, even if it has been tightly woven into the other functions we have discussed.

In a paper prepared for the United Church of Christ reflecting on the just peace church, M. Douglas Meeks writes that the just peace church will make it clear to its members and to fellow citizens that making peace is not a technical, scientific, and political question to be entrusted to experts. Resisting the notion that esoteric or clandestine knowledge can save us or authorize the few to make decisions of war and peace for the many, Meeks says that the just peace church will insist that peace is the responsibility of the individual person acting as a citizen. It will empower its people for responsible citizenship and will actively enter into the effort in a corporate way.

Meeks also notes that the just peace church will uncover the real threats to national security that are posed by economic and social injustice and by the hostaging of the economy to pay for a global military network. It "will make realistic arguments at every conceivable opportunity against the notion that increased defense spending and armaments can bring greater security to the nation and world. . . . It will do everything in its power to demonstrate that . . . a new order of security must be based on economic justice, political freedom, and cultural unity in diversity."[14]

A peacemaking congregation will educate and advocate in these matters. Its members will engage in legislative action, writing letters to their congresspersons. The congregation will network within the denomination as well as with other groups and coalitions. Some members will be called by conscience to respond with protest and resistance, whether it be public vigils, civil disobedience, tax resistance, or conscientious objection to selective service. The just parish will respect and support these people. And finally, in the church where spiritual security has taken deep root so that vulnerability, compassion, and solidarity are deeply experienced qualities, there will be corporate acts of protest and resistance. Churches offering sanctuary to people fleeing political violence in South Africa and Central America exemplify this sense of true spiritual security.

The just peace church will seek to come to terms with U.S./U.S.S.R. enmity. There must be no denial of the abuse of human rights and political freedom in the Soviet Union and work must continue to address these wrongs. Furthermore, the suffering and displacement of families caused by the U.S.S.R.'s invasion of Afghanistan should be understood to be as painful as the misery visited upon Nicaraguans by the U.S.-backed Contra forces. Compassion knows no national boundaries. At the same time, the just peacemaking congregation will reject thinking in stereotypic ways about the Russian people, and it will be open to hopeful signs in the new Soviet leadership. It will seek to develop an appreciation for the people and history of the Soviet Union through education, Peace Bridge projects, travel, and people-to-people programs. Political action will be an outgrowth, for when congregations can begin thinking of the enemy in human terms as grandparents, toddlers, and sweethearts who share many of our same hopes and fears, the requirements of the gospel will confront our enmity. Legislation on the defense budget and nuclear testing, for example, will be understood as directly connected to the welfare of people and families living in Russia and the Soviet states.

To say that political and social engagement by the peacemaking congregation must occur in order to weave a completed pattern is not to say that it is to be expected that all or even most of the members will directly participate in the responses that flow through this function, although an offering of letters is something in which many could share. Some will never be comfortable with direct involvement, although they will participate in some other aspect of the church's peacemaking and perhaps grow into political witness and action. Others will not participate because they are fearful of it or simply are against "mixing politics and religion." In the case of fearfulness we come full circle to earlier discussions, rediscovering the imperative for the congregation to address the causes of insecurity, fear, and defensiveness within its own body. In the case of those angered or in disagreement with a church being involved in political action, the peacemaking congregation will seek to be "a community of honest and open conflict, a zone of freedom where differences may be expressed, explored, and worked through in mutual understanding and growth."[15]

The central issue is not how many participate in the political and social engagement of peace and justice. What is fundamental is that God's call to struggle and respond to these questions of faithfulness be willingly owned by the pastor, lay leaders, and governing body. The importance of authorization cannot be overemphasized. Nor can the singular importance of the role of the pastor be denied.

The Catholic bishops take note of this, saying, "This letter will be known by the faithful only as well as you know it, preach and teach it, and use it creatively."[16] The letters and pronouncements by all denominations on peace and justice need to be known, preached, taught, and used creatively by their respective pastors. Citing peacemaking as a sacred calling from Jesus, the Council of Bishops of the United Methodist Church reiterates this: "We call upon each local pastor and lay leader to give leadership in a local church study of the issues surrounding the nuclear threat."[17]

When authorization for the willingness to struggle is established, what issues will a congregation consider? The Presbyterian Peacemaking Program is helpful in the way it frames the responses of a peacemaking congregation, suggesting the following areas for planning:[18]

Domestic Justice

A peacemaking congregation will help the people to work for social, racial, and economic justice, and it will respond to people in the community who are caught in poverty, hurt by unemployment, or burdened by other problems. (As discussed in the previous section, this can occur in part through the church's institutional lifestyle.)

Global Justice and Human Rights

A peacemaking congregation will encourage the people to support human rights and economic justice efforts *in at least one area of the world*, such as Central America, Southern Africa, the Middle East, East Asia, East Europe, or Central Asia.

The Arms Race and Militarism

A peacemaking congregation will work to help end the arms race, to reverse the worldwide growth of militarism, and to reduce tension among nations. Having specific, identifiable goals and projects will enable the church to act on this.

Deciding the "what" and "how" of the church's peacemaking program needs to be carefully considered. There is an abundance of excellent resources available that will be helpful, both in the examination of the issues and in the processes for leading people from study and discernment to witness and action.[19]

As a Peace Task Force begins to discern an appropriate course of action, these are some items to think about:

— Select issues or areas of study and action that suggest there is a constituency for that issue and local resource persons available, if possible, who can share their experience or expertise. Recognize that people who are confused about matters of faith intersecting with government policy probably represent a constituency.

—Limit the number of issues, selecting those that present the opportunity to turn the study into some type of meaningful action. Take one step at a time, taking care not to overwhelm people. The chairperson of the task force of a congregation in Hinsdale, Illinois put it this way: "You have to narrow down to the issues you can handle and where you think you can make a difference."

— Be aware of the effect of semantics. Avoid rhetoric, jargon, and emotionally loaded words; they will not help you one iota. Speak the truth in love, drawing on the experiences of people, the data available to you, and biblical and theological reflections.

—Choose speakers and leaders who speak the truth responsibly and sensitively. Leaders need to be well informed. Also, careful attention to group process is imperative. Many of us have learned from painful mistakes that this cannot be overlooked. You are dealing with fears, deep feelings, and long-cherished traditions of patriotism. Peace and justice cannot be advanced by denying who people are.

— Remember you are working *with* people *about* issues. Create opportunities for fellowship, celebrate victories, and plan for some fun. Don't overload or lay on guilt. Set realistic and achieveable goals that respect the finiteness of people's time and energies, and also their personal needs. Affirm their efforts and staying power. Challenge them to new visions. Value relationships and community, even as you work through your disagreements.

Called to Faithfulness

Finally, let us remember that our call is to be faithful to God's will for justice and righteousness, which may or may not include being "successful" in some program or project. It is not ours to know when we have been able to help someone interpret reality in a new way or to know when we have helped change some part of the established order. To have the need to validate the significance of our efforts by seeing the results that we had hoped for by the time we had planned to see them is to forget that God is still in charge.

Mother Teresa has spoken of being a pencil in God's hand. Remembering this metaphor, we can get beyond our timid and narrow visions that are limited by our egos and fearfulness, opening ourselves to the urgings of the Spirit. God does not say "Plan a successful study series." Rather, God asks of us fidelity and courage to venture into the unknown, so that the security of God's *shalom* might become the known reality of hearts, relationships, and nations.

"*You did not choose me; I chose you and appointed you to go and bear much fruit, the kind of fruit that endures*" (John 15:16).

14

"Now, Go!"

"*But Moses said, 'No* Lord, *don't send me. . . . I have never been a good speaker. . . .' The* Lord *said to him, 'Who gives man his mouth? Who makes him deaf or dumb? Who gives him sight or makes him blind? It is I, the* Lord. *Now, go! I will help you to speak, and I will tell you what to say.' But Moses answered, 'No, Lord, please send someone else'* " (Exodus 4:10-13).

We have spent this time together, imagining a different reality from the one that is ever-present in our lives through advertising, the air waves, corporate strategies, and a national security state. As the principalities and powers sell packages of strength, envy, independence, and superiority, the glitz of the wrappings bedazzle, blinding us to the emptiness, loneliness, violence, and despair that are wrapped inside.

Amidst the distractions, distortions, and social chaos of Caesar's order comes another voice, gentle but compelling, saying, "I give you a new commandment: love one another. As I have loved you, so you must love one another. . . . There is no fear in love; perfect love drives out all fear. . . . Peace is what I leave with you; it is my own peace that I give you. I do not give it as the world does. Do not be worried and upset; do not be afraid" (John 13:34; 1 John 4:18; John 14:27).

And you and I, imagining a vision of wholeness, harmony, justice, and well-being for all God's people, find ourselves present to both realities. We believe we have heard and answered the call to peacemaking, only to be confronted with our own inconsistencies. We have set about to break the cycles of fear that spiral forth into violence, only to find that defensiveness is still alive and well within our own hearts. We make a few steps in our values of mutuality and solidarity, only to come face to face with our fierce needs to own and control. Brueggemann's confession is our own:

> Both the church with its vision and the world with its fear are here today, and they are in our guts. I am tangled up with the values and priorities of the world and so are you; it cannot be otherwise. Part of the hatred of the world toward church is within my own body and yours. It has to do with the coerced parts of my person in conflict with the vision of joy that sustains me. And that conflict tears at me. We are . . . making up our minds about that deep conflict between yearning for *shalom* and yet wanting business with the world to continue uninterrupted. You and I will not likely rush madly to that new vision of confidence, but it is possible for folks like us to keep the tension alive.[1]

Some will look at a congregation's vision to honor God's reign through spiritual conversion and reconciled relationships as it works for a nation of justice and a world at peace, saying, "Yeah, but. . . . " We have all heard the litany of the "Yeah, but's." Too many times we have been intimidated by their words of cynicism without being open to their feelings of fear, powerlessness, and despair. As people who have been claimed, loved, forgiven, and accepted, we must continue to bring the vision of hope and love, finding ways to do justice, restore true security, and reconcile the estranged.

Some say that peacemakers are foolish to risk and invest in imagining another reality. People imagining a new life take chances every day, whether it be on the lottery, the stock market, or a new fast-food franchise. And as our nation mortgages its future, betting on the security of Star Wars, we are reminded that imagining and investing in what others call the improbable is not unique to the peacemakers. So we will not apologize for our foolishness.

Martin Luther King, Jr. was told that he was foolish to imagine that blacks would someday be guaranteed by law their civil rights. How preposterous to imagine that drinking fountains could someday be accessible to all! And what foolish dreamer could have imagined that Cory Aquino, a grandmother with no political experience, would inspire the Filipinos to bring down the entrenched and brutal Marcos government with nonviolence? Impossible! These are testimonies to love's foolishness. Seeing the suffering Christ in others, these people abandoned fear and acted in the confidence of God's love. Their witness teaches that we, too, can venture out on our faith, trusting in the enabling power of the Holy Spirit as we share in God's continuing work among us.

The time is now, the place is where we find ourselves; the questions are difficult and many. What do I fear? What cuts me off from joy, coercing me to do what I would not, and not do what I would?[2] What changes can I make to free myself for servanthood and vulnerability? With whom can I reconcile? What deeds of justice will I risk? In what way will I resist the waging of war? If my peacemaking comes down to putting one foot in front of the other, what is the very next step that I will take?

And the Lord said, Go!
and I said, Who, me?
and God said, Yes, you!
and I said, But I'm not ready yet
and there is company coming,
and I can't leave my kids;
You know there's no one to take my place.
And God said, You're stalling.

Again the Lord said, Go!
and I said, But I don't want to,
and God said, I didn't ask if you wanted to.
And I said, Listen, I'm not the kind of person
to get involved in controversy.
Besides, my family won't like it,
and what will the neighbors think!
And God said, Baloney!

And yet a third time the Lord said, Go!
and I said, Do I have to?
and God said, Do you love me?
and I said, Look, I'm scared. . . .
People are going to hate me . . .
and cut me up into little pieces . . .
I can't take it all by myself.
And God said, Where do you think I'll be?

And the Lord said, Go!
and I sighed,
Here I am, send me![3]

Epilogue

"Then I saw a new heaven and a new earth. . . . *I heard a loud voice call from the throne, 'Look, here God lives among human beings. He will make* his home among them; they will be his people, *and he will be their God,* God-with-them. He will wipe *away all* tears from their eyes*; there will be no more death, and no more mourning or sadness or pain. The world of the past is gone.' Then the One sitting on the throne spoke. 'Look, I am making the whole of creation new'"* (Revelation 21:1, 3-5, NJB).

God is just and righteous; Jesus is our Redeemer, claiming us and healing all brokenness. Secure in this gracious love and strengthened by the Spirit, let us say Yes to God's power for life. Let us now journey in love, courage, and nonviolence, breaking the cycles of fear that breed war, chaos, and injustice; acting in faithfulness to help God create a new reality when preparations for battle will cease and all "will live in peace among [their] own vineyards and fig trees, and no one will make [them] afraid" (Micah 4:4, adapted).

> May the love of God, the peace of Christ, and the power of the Holy Spirit be among you, everywhere and always, so that you may be a blessing to all creation and to all the children of God, making peace and remembering the poor, choosing life and coming to life eternal, in God's own good time.[1]
>
> Amen.

A Symbol for Christian Peacemaking

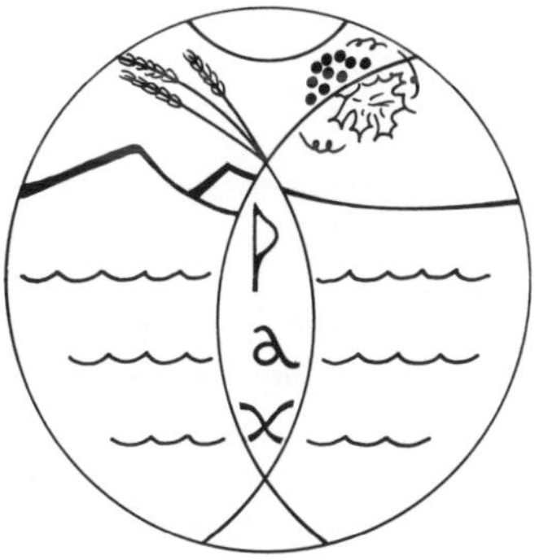

Beginning with the sign of the fish used by the early Christians, this symbol of Christian peacemaking suggests that our peacemaking is centered in Christ, whose life, death, and resurrection are God's gift of grace and peace to the world. The grapes and branches recall Christ's new commandment to live in his love: "I am the vine, and you are the branches. Whoever remains in me, and I in him, will bear much fruit; for you can do nothing without me" (John 15:5). The wheat affirms that justice is the bread of peace, giving life to God's love in the structures of a just society. The staffs of wheat number three: for Sovereign God, the author of peace; Son Jesus, the gift of peace; and the Spirit, who is the helper for our peacemaking.

The sun, earth, mountains, and water speak of God's life-giving creation and of God's active presence in history. The arcs and circular motif represent reconciliation and harmony amongst humankind and with the earth.

Artist: Ann Currinder

Notes

Chapter 1

1. *Webster's New Collegiate Dictionary*. S. & C. Merriam & Company, 1981, pp. 415, 592.

2. Jim Wallis, ed., *Waging Peace: A Handbook for the Struggle to Abolish Nuclear Weapons*. Harper & Row, 1982, p. 6.

3. Walter Brueggemann, *Living Toward a Vision: Biblical Reflections on Shalom*. United Church Press, 1976, 1982, pp. 42, 43, 163.

4. The Hebrew word *shalom* and the Greek word *eirene* are appropriately translated "peace" in many of their uses in the Bible. Discussion of the differences, nuances, and complements of *shalom* and *eirene* are beyond the scope of this notation. Suffice it to say that *eirene* most often refers to relationships between God and the believer, and among believers within the church. *Shalom* is "harmony and justice in human relationships, the security of life, the health of body and mind, and the enjoyment of a beneficial and nondestructive realm of nature" (Gowan and Mauser). For a helpful theological discussion of the two words, see the paper "Shalom and Eirene," by Donald E. Gowan and Ulrich W. Mauser in *The Peacemaking Struggle: Militarism and Resistance*, Stone and Wilbanks, eds., University Press of America, 1985, pp. 123-133.

Chapter 2

1. A nuclear first-strike policy took form in the early 1950s as the preemptive first strike doctrine, whereby nuclear weapons were to be used against the Soviet nation in retaliation for unwanted Soviet conventional moves in Europe. In 1962, during the Kennedy administration, Secretary of State Robert McNamara outlined a strategy for "counterforce" that sounded humane, for its objective was the destruction of the enemy's military forces and missile silos rather than the civilian population, keeping the death toll "to a minimum."

In fact, counterforce is a synonym for first-strike, for it is of no military value to destroy empty silos if the missiles themselves have already been dispatched. The essential requirement of counterforce is that U.S. missiles and bombers be aloft and near target before the enemy is aware, so that a first-strike can be achieved. Furthermore, the strategy's claim to humaneness by destroying "the enemy's military forces, not the civilian population," knocking out the missiles while still in their silos, ignores the widespread environmental implications of a single atomic strike. The accident at Chernobyl in 1986 brought this significance to international attention.

American presidents have repeatedly refused to deny the first-strike option. It is still in place today, even though the Soviets have pledged not to use nuclear weapons first. For a history of the arms race see Sidney Lens, *The Day Before Doomsday*. Beacon Press, 1977. For an assessment of the arms race in the 80s, see Helen Caldicott, *Missile Envy*. Bantam Books, rev. 1986.

2. John Francis Kavanaugh, *Following Christ in a Consumer Society: The Spirituality of Cultural Resistance*. Orbis Books, 1983. See discussion of thing-knowledge and thing-values; pp. 21-62.

Chapter 3

1. Sam Keen, *Faces of the Enemy — Reflections on the Hostile Imagination*. Harper & Row, 1986. pp. 11, 19.
2. *St. Louis Post-Dispatch*, August 9, 1986.
3. See the writings of Abraham Maslow; in particular *The Farther Reaches of Human Nature*. Viking Press, 1971; and *Motivation and Personality*. Harper & Row, 1970.
4. Henri Nouwen, "The Spirituality of Peacemaking." *The Lutheran*, February 5, 1986, p. 14.
5. Alfred C. Krass, *Pastoring for Peace and Justice*. Jubilee Inc., 1986. p. 5.

Chapter 4

1. James McGinnis, *Bread and Justice: Toward a New International Economic Order*. Paulist Press, 1979, p. 9.
2. *Ibid.*, p. 10.
3. Robert McAfee Brown, *Saying Yes and Saying No: On Rendering to God and Caesar*. Westminster Press, 1986, p. 61.
4. Ruth Leger Sivard, *World Military and Social Expenditures — 1985*. World Priorities, 1985. Gives excellent overview. New edition annually.
5. Gerald and Patricia Mische, *Toward a Human World Order: Beyond the National Security Straitjacket*. Paulist Press, 1977, p. 40.
6. Martin Luther King, Jr., *The Trumpet of Conscience*. Harper & Row, 1967, pp. 69, 70.
7. M. Douglas Meeks, Lecture at Eden Theological Seminary, St. Louis, October, 1984.

8. Elaine Saum, *How Should Christians Be Involved in the Public Arena? A Study Guide for Presbyterian Congregations*. Presbyterian Peacemaking Program, n.d., p. 2.

Chapter 5

1. Henri Nouwen, *From the House of Fear to the House of Love*, cassette tape. Paulist Press, 1983.
2. Kavanaugh discusses the commodity society, where marketing and consuming infiltrate every aspect of our lives and where competition, domination, and violence result. See Kavanaugh, *Following Christ in a Consumer Society*, pp. 27-48.
3. Wallis, *Waging Peace*, p. 195.
4. Kavanaugh, *Following Christ in a Consumer Society*, p. 122. Adapted.
5. Jürgen Moltmann, *Theology of Hope*. SCM Press, n.d., p. 21.
6. Attributed.
7. William E. Gibson, "Confessing and Covenanting." *Shalom Connections in Personal and Congregational Life*, ed. by Dieter Hessel. Program Agency, Presbyterian Church (U.S.A.), 1986, p.21.
8. *Ibid*.
9. Allan Boesak, *Walking on Thorns: The Call to Christian Obedience*. Eerdmans, 1984, p.41.

Chapter 6

1. The phrase "parenting for peace and justice" comes from the book of that name by Kathleen and James McGinnis (Orbis, 1981), which opened a new area of consciousness for the peace and justice movement.
2. Diane Perlman, *Humanizing the Enemy and Ourselves*. Peace Research Associates, March, 1986, p. 16.
3. Ram Dass, *Grist for the Mill*. Unity Press, 1977.

Chapter 7

1. Peter J. Henriot, S. J., "The Love that Does Justice." *Center Focus*, Issue 74, August, 1986. p. 3.
2. Brown, *Saying Yes and Saying No*, p. 55.
3. John Francis Kavanaugh, speaking at Eden Theological Seminary, April 13, 1986.
4. Phillip Russell, retiring Anglican Archbishop of Capetown, S. Africa, interviewed on "The World of Religion," CBS Radio, September 7, 1986.

5. Gibson, see discussion on pp. 21, 22.

6. Milo Thornberry, "Celebrating." *Shalom Connections in Personal and Congregational Life*, ed. by Dieter Hessel. Program Agency, Presbyterian Church (U.S.A.), 1986, p. 90.

7. There are many fine resources to help in forming a more conscientious lifestyle including Hessel, ed., *Shalom Connections in Personal and Congregational Life*, Alternatives; Doris Janzen Longacre, *Living More with Less* and *The More with Less Cookbook*, Herald Press; *To Celebrate—Reshaping Holidays and Rites of Passage,* Alternatives, 1987; Marilyn Helmuth Voran, *Add Justice to Your Shopping List*, Herald Press, 1986.

8. "Naming the Poor" from *Seeds*, April, 1981 as quoted in *Suggestions for Implementing the "Commitment to Peacemaking."* Presbyterian Peacemaking Program of the Presbyterian Church (U.S.A.), p. 49.

9. For further information contact Quest for Peace, c/o the Quixote Center, P.O. Box 5206, Hyattsville, MD 20782.

10. C. Watts, et al, "Domestic Justice Think Piece." *Suggestions for Implementing the "Commitment to Peacemaking."*

Chapter 8

1. Wasserman, Darion, and Leigh, *Man of La Mancha*. Dell, 1968, p. 99.

2. William Robert Miller, from *The Round Table,* a journal of the St. Louis Catholic Worker, Autumn, 1986, p. 21.

3. *National Catholic Reporter*, March 22, 1985, special supplement.

4. American Friends National Legislative Hotline, (202) 547-4343; Anti-apartheid Action Hotline, (202) 546-0408; Central America Legislative Hotline, (202) 543-0664; Interfaith Action for Economic Justice (800) 424-7292; Nuclear Arms Control (202) 543-0006.

5. Miller, *The Round Table*.

6. Moltmann, *Theology of Hope*.

Chapter 10

1. Patricia Washburn and Robert Gribbon, *Peacemaking Without Division: Moving Beyond Congregational Apathy and Anger*. The Alban Institute, 1986, p. 3.

2. *Ibid.*, p. 7.

3. Attributed.

4. Krass, *Pastoring for Peace and Justice*, p. 2.

5. *Webster's New Collegiate Dictionary*. S. & C. Merriam & Co., 1981, p. 833.

6. Krass, *Pastoring for Peace and Justice*, pp. 6, 7.
7. Sivard, *World Military and Social Expenditures—1985*, p. 5.
8. Brown, *Saying Yes and Saying No*, p. 44.

Chapter 11

1. Thornberry, p. 96.
2. Bartlett and Hessel, "Empowering." *Shalom Connections in Personal and Congregational Life*, ed. by Dieter Hessel. Program Agency, Presbyterian Church (U.S.A.), 1986, p. 117.

Chapter 12

1. See the four-session Bible study series, *Dealing with Conflict in the Congregation,* Presbyterian Peacemaking Program. Available from Presbyterian Distribution Service, 905 Interchurch Center, 475 Riverside Dr., New York, NY 10115.
2. Thornberry, p. 94.
3. Richard Watts, "Peacemaking and Worship." *Suggestions for Implementing the Commitment to Peacemaking*, p. 11.
4. *Ibid.*, adapted from pp. 11, 12.
5. R. Blair Moffett, "Worshiping as Peacemaking." *Peacemaking in Your Congregation*, Presbyterian Peacemaking Project, 1982, p. 12.
6. Some of the suggestions come from the articles by Watts and Moffett above.
7. Ron Kraybill, *Managing Conflict Cassette Workshop*. Mennonite Conciliation Service, 1985, Sec. V-E.
8. This quote, from a longer paraphrase by Rabbi Robert Jacobs, is derived from an ancient commentary on Exodus 15 in the Midrashic literature.
9. See Questionnaires 1 and 2 in Holland and Henriot. *Social Analysis: Linking Faith with Justice* (Orbis, rev. 1983) for beginning social analysis and evaluating social action responses.
10. James McGinnis, "Towards Compassionate and Courageous Action." *Religious Education*, Vol. 81, No. 3.
11. Excellent materials for parishes wishing to address hunger are available from Bread for the World, 802 Rhode Island Ave. NE, Washington, D.C. 20018.

Chapter 13

1. Excerpts of a few of the many valuable comments received from thirty-eight respondents to a survey I made on the status of peacemaking

in congregations of eight denominations in various parts of the country in 1986.

2. Speed Leas, *Moving Your Church Through Conflict* (1984) and *A Lay Person's Guide to Conflict Management* (1979), Alban Institute; video tape and consulting from Mennonite Conciliation Service, M.C.C., Akron, PA 17501.

3. Parenting for Peace & Justice Network, 4144 Lindell, #122, St. Louis, MO 63108.

4. See *Parents' Guide to Non-Violent Toy Buying*. Discipleship Resources, UMC, Box 189, Nashville, TN 37202.

5. Andrew Fluegelman, ed., *The New Games Book*. New Games Foundation, Box 7901, San Francisco, CA 94120.

6. National Interreligious Service Board for Conscientious Objectors (NISBCO), 800 80th St. NW, #600, Washington, D.C. 20006; program aids from Institute for Peace & Justice, 4144 Lindell, #122, St. Louis, MO 63108.

7. Jubilee Crafts, 300 W. Apsley St., Philadelphia, PA 19144. Also SERRV, Mennonites Self Help; others.

8. Report of the 1979 Mission Consultation, 118th General Assembly of the Presbyterian Church in the U.S. as quoted in McGinnis, *Parenting for Peace and Justice*. Orbis, 1981, p. 7.

9. Doris Janzen Longacre, *Living More with Less*. Herald Press, 1980, p. 231.

10. Interfaith Center on Corporate Responsibility, Room 566, 475 Riverside Drive, New York, NY 10115.

11. National Conference of Catholic Bishops, *The Challenge of Peace: God's Promise and Our Response,* 1983, p. 73.

12. The United Methodist Council of Bishops, *In Defense of Creation — The Nuclear Crisis and a Just Peace*, pastoral letter. Graded Press, 1986.

13. National Conference of Catholic Bishops, *The Challenge of Peace*, p. 87.

14. M. Douglas Meeks, *Reflections on the United Church of Christ as a Peace Church*. Office for Church in Society, U.C.C.

15. United Church of Christ, *Pronouncement Affirming the United Church of Christ as a Just Peace Church*, IV-B.

16. National Conference of Catholic Bishops, *The Challenge of Peace*, p. 92.

17. The United Methodist Council of Bishops, *In Defense of Creation*.

18. Presbyterian Church (U.S.A.), *Suggestions for Implementing the "Commitment to Peacemaking"*. Presbyterian Peacemaking Program, p. 3.

19. Check with your denomination's peacemaking office or program. For resources of an ecumenical nature in Parenting for Peace and Justice and in Educating for Peace and Justice contact the Institute for Peace & Justice, 4144 Lindell, #122, St. Louis, MO 63108.

Chapter 14

1. Brueggemann, *Living Toward a Vision*, p. 121.
2. See Brueggemann's discussion of the Shalom Person, *Living Toward a Vision*, p. 163.
3. "The Lord said, 'Go' " from *Maryknoll* magazine; a poem read by Lois Hodrick during a Maryknoll Mission Institute, New York. My gratitude is extended to the unknown author.

Epilogue

1. The United Methodist Council of Bishops, *In Defense of Creation*.